BUILDING YOUR
SPIRITUAL CORE

BUILDING YOUR SPIRITUAL CORE

101 Creative Ways to Connect with God

Ron Parrish

Partnership
Publications

A Division of House to House Publications

Building Your Spiritual Core
101 Creative Ways to Connect with God

by Ron Parrish

Copyright © 2016 by Ron Parrish

ISBN-10: 0-9962924-8-9
ISBN-13: 978-0-9962924-8-1

Published by
Partnership Publications
11 Toll Gate Road
Lititz, PA 17543 USA
A Division of House to House Publications
www.H2HP.com

Dedication

I wish to dedicate this book to a group of people who believe in Janine and I and what we are doing so much that they sacrifice a portion of their hard-earned income to make it possible for us to live and serve in Indonesia – our support team. What an incredible commitment you've made to us! At least a dozen of you have been under our pastoral leadership for two decades. Some of you we barely know, yet you believe in our vision. Most of you have known us as your pastors for at least some season of your life. We have been deeply humbled by your voluntary, generous, and consistent support for the last five years. Thank you seems so inadequate. We honor your faithfulness in our lives and want everyone who reads this book to know that in a tangible way you made it possible. Chunks of time to compile these exercises came during these last five years between our work of initiating, training, and coaching people for church planting movements. We owe you a debt of love.

May your investment in us result in all of us presenting to the Lamb the reward of His suffering on that Great Day!

Acknowledgements

I am extremely grateful for the people who have made this idea a reality. First, for my wife Janine, who graciously gave me time and space to research, create, and field test these exercises and then labor through the process of writing out the insights I had discovered. You sacrificed many hours for my devotion to this project. Thank you.

I am forever indebted to my friend Mike O'Quin Jr. who corrected at least 777 grammar and spelling mistakes in my first draft. More significantly, he gave me invaluable feedback on the content. He not only encouraged me but also graciously pushed back when I communicated something that was not my intent, because he's known me for twenty-three years.

Diane Omondi, my professional editor took the book to a whole new level on the second edit. Thanks Diane. You are brilliant, yet a servant!

Jackson Robinson from Kings Wild Project designed the book cover. Thanks for serving me. You really ARE a redneck artist, with the emphasis on artist.

Finally, Sarah Suader from Partnership Publications is my publisher who treats me like a loyal friend. Sarah, this is the second time I have looked to you for help to put into a print some ideas that I felt were God-inspired. Each time you came through, big time. Thank you for believing in me, and trusting me. You have made this dream a reality.

CONTENTS

Introduction 13

  1. A Prayer Journal 21

Exercises that Cultivate Gratitude 25

  2. Count Your Blessings 26

  3. Focused Gratitude 29

  4. Turning Stress into Gratitude. 31

  5. Gratitude for People 33

  6. Join in the Blessings of Others 35

  7. Creating Your Own Psalm of Gratitude 37

  8. Turning Bible Reading into Prayers of Gratitude... 39

  9. Thanking God for Health 42

 10. One Thousand Gifts 44

 11. God's Provision 46

 12. Thanking God for Hearing Us. 48

Exercises that Help Us Worship 51

 13. Awestruck by the Size of God 52

 14. The Names of God and Jesus 54

 15. The ABC's of Adoration 56

 16. God, I have Found You to Be… 58

 17. Before the Throne 60

 18. A Love Letter 62

 19. A Love Song 64

 20. Dancing Before the Lord 66

 21. Worship with Instruments 68

 22. Borrowing from the Prayers of Others 70

 23. Shout Out Your Praise 72

 24. Praising God for What He has Made 74

7

Exercises in Surrender 77
25. Our Bodies—His Temple 78
26. Offer Physical Assets to God........................ 80
27. Offer Intangible Assets to God 82
28. Obedience-Based Discipleship 84

Exercises that Free us from Guilt and Shame 87
29. Forgiven.. 88
30. A Clean Slate 90
31. Silencing the Lies.. 92
32. Addressing Hurtful Memories....................... 94

Exercises That Help Us Experience God's Love 97
33. Experiencing God's Love Through the Cross 98
35. Bathed in an Ocean of God's Love 100
36. Transforming Your Mental Image of God............ 102
37. Picture God This Way.................................. 105
38. A Breath of Life.. 107
39. Revelations of God's Love............................ 108

Exercises That Overcome Anxiety and Stress 111
40. Palms Up, Palms Down, Palms Up 112
41. Telling God How You Feel............................ 114
42. Cast Your Cares on HIM 116
43. A Christian Mantra...................................... 118
44. A Biblical Sabbath 120

Exercises that Bring Us Faith to ASK 123
45. Top Ten Answered Prayers........................... 124
46. Praying with Gall.. 126
47. Persistent Prayer 129
48. Images of the Longings of Your Heart............. 131
49. A 21-Day PUSH 133
50. Expressing Your Disappointments.................. 135

51. Praying the Promises 137
52. Being Honest About Your Doubts 139
53. The Things I Want Most in Life 142

Exercises That Bring Us Joy 145
54. Joyful Memories 146
55. Drilling Down into a Joyful Memory 148
56. A Prayer for More Joy 150
57. Activate HOPE 152
58. What I Have to Look Forward To 154
59. Laughing at the Lies 156

Exercises that Bring Us Freedom 157
60. A Beginner's Fast 158
61. Celebrating Freedom 160
62. Power to Resist Temptation 162
63. The Freedom of a Clean Conscience 165
64. A Fast from Your Electronic Devices 168

Exercises that Help Us Listen 171
65. A Silent Retreat 172
66. If God were Speaking to Me 174
67. Discerning God's Counsel 176

Exercises that Cultivate a Sense of God's Presence 179
68. A Mind Fixed on Christ 180
69. A Running Conversation with God 182
70. Practicing His Presence 184
71. The Daily Office 186

Exercises in Praying the Bible 189
72. Prayers of the Bible 190
73. Knowing God Through Jesus 192
74. Bible Immersion 194

75. Bible Reading into Prayer.................................... 196
76. Taking Part in the Narrative.............................. 198
77. Life Transformation Groups 200
78. Meditating on Scripture—One verse.................. 202
79. Memorizing and Meditating on
    Scripture —Large Chunks................................ 204
80. Praying Acts.. 206

Igniting Passion in Prayer 209
81. Praying with Divine Passion............................ 210
82. Korean-Style Prayer.. 213
83. Kingdom of God Come, Will of God Be Done.... 215
84. Prayers that Exercise Authority........................ 218
85. A Prayer for Healing.. 221

Praying for People Far from God 225
86. A Heart of Compassion.................................... 226
87. Praying Jesus' Final Command......................... 229
88. Your Most Wanted List.................................... 231
89. Prayer Triplets... 233
90. Praying for Missionaries.................................. 235
91. 10/40 Window Prayer....................................... 238
92. Praying for Muslims... 241
93. Praying for Hindus... 244

Other Kinds of Spiritual Exercises 247
94. Praying Biographies: Bible Heroes.................... 248
95. Praying Biographies: Church History Heroes 250
96. Crafted Prayers 252
97. A Crafted Prayer for My Spouse....................... 254
98. Highs and Lows of My Day.............................. 256
99. Who God Says I Am 257
100. Destiny Revelation Experiences 259
101. Discerning God's Purpose for My Life.................. 262

Endnotes 265

Bibliography 268

Appendix A
ABC's of Adoration 270

Appendix B
An Example of Promises 271

Appendix C
Some of My Crafted Prayers 272

Appendix D
My True Identity in Christ – examples 275

Introduction

I know this about many people I know. They don't pray as much as they want to. Sometimes it's a point of guilt or shame because they know they really ought to pray more. The more we feel guilty about not praying enough, the less likely we are to see prayer as something that is life-giving. Most of us really want to live close to God. It's just that the frenetic pace of our lives, the demands of work and family, the attachment to our electronic devices, and maybe even the busyness of our social (or church) calendars do not leave a lot of discretionary time for pursuing an authentic, meaningful, spirituality. If we are completely honest, we will admit that our attempts to establish some kind of consistent, meaningful devotional life that is life-giving is illusive. Perhaps our attempts are too feeble. Perhaps our devotional times have become too boring. If any of these is the case, this book is for you. Perhaps we just don't know exactly what we should do when we do carve out time to pray. If that's the case, this book really is for you.

Like you, I have struggled with having a deep and meaningful spiritual life. But I am convinced it's worth the struggle, because what I have experienced on the other side of that struggle is so amazingly sweet and delightful that I would climb any mountain of apathy to get there. The view from the top is stunning. I can honestly say that now I love spending focused time pouring out my heart to God for me and others. I love expressing my gratitude and adoration He so clearly deserves. I love trying to get to know Him through His Word. I love experiencing His presence. The first one to two hours every morning connecting with Him are a "get to" for me. I love to take a walk through a forest (there are jungles where I live) with Him on a cool afternoon after a thunderstorm. I love walking out under a canopy of stars and being awestruck at the size of God's heavens. My life is a testimony of how God can capture our affections by transforming dull, routine, check-the-box quiet times into daily life-giving encounters with Him.

I covet the same for you.

Yes, as the title of this book implies, there are actually a hundred and one different ways we can connect with God that I have compiled here. You probably have practiced some of these exercises, but you won't be familiar with all of them because some are my original creations. Many have been practiced by devotional masters from past centuries. *All* have been field tested. Not all of them will inspire you or help you feel closer to God, but out of these 101 exercises I'm hoping there will be many that do—many that rock your devotional life world.

Let me warn you before you get started: this is not a Christian teaching book, an inspirational book, or even a book *about* prayer. Technically, it's not even a book that you would want to sit down and read from cover to cover. It's more like a prayer manual. But it's not the kind of prayer manual in which you pray someone else's prayers. In these exercises, you will have to create your own prayers. View these exercises as just that, a spiritual workout. You will be challenged to be an active participant in these pages, encountering the Living God, rather than passively receiving the predigested thoughts of others. Honestly, this manual will have little value if you plan on reading it like a book. However, through engaging with these exercises, God will seem much more real to you than He does right now.

I am a firm believer that nothing will be as valuable to your prayer life as actually praying—**we learn by doing**. Inspirational thoughts on prayer don't translate into developing a lifestyle of prayer. The things that motivate us to pray are positive, life-giving prayer experiences. "Feel" the empowering presence of God as you pour out your heart to Him and you will want to pray more. "Hear" God's words of comfort, encouragement, or affirmation and you'll have no problem crawling out of bed earlier tomorrow to get more time with Him. When at the end of a prayer time you feel more peaceful, more joyful, more light-hearted, more confident, and more aware of God's love, you have learned much more about prayer than you would have by digesting a dozen books on prayer. When you practice prayer, God's personal love for you moves from just a doctrine you believe to an experience that touches the depth of your emotions.

If you are married and have made serious efforts toward cultivating intimacy in your relationship with your spouse, the value of these spiritual exercises will make sense. You know that you can hear or read tons of information about marriage, but a conversation in which you communicate with each other on a heart level is worth far more than being taught helpful marriage principles. Even more valuable is to put yourself in a setting in which you are encouraged (or directed) to talk about things you don't normally talk about. Have you ever been guided into experiencing intimacy in your marriage on multiple levels in a safe, private, and healthy environment by a couple who have a super healthy relationship and who have been married a long time? Janine and I have had the privilege of taking part in various marriage trainings that have pushed us toward meaningful interaction. Compare that to sitting and passively listening to a seminar on how to make your marriage better.

Let me use this marriage illustration to further explain the approach of this book. The couple engaging in the marriage exercises would not have as their goal simply making sure that they do the exercises well. They know that their relationship is the goal. They want to *experience* each other so as to enhance their love for each other and their spiritual, emotional and physical intimacy. The exercises are a means to that end. Furthermore, if the couple were to add some creative ideas to the "assignments" from the marriage guru, that would be quite okay. The goal is to *experience* each other so as to enhance their love for each other. The couple also knows that the desired outcome of the marriage weekend is a change in their lifestyle. What would really be healthy for their marriage would be to keep working on enhancing their intimacy through practicing ways that help them connect.

We could also illustrate the spiritual training dynamic of the exercises in this manual from the world of physical training. That's why I titled this book, "Building Your Spiritual Core." You're probably familiar with core building if you have read fitness books. My friend Jeff taught me how to build my core. He did me a favor that has affected my health in ways that I could never repay. He took an afternoon at the gym to walk me through a dozen core-building exercises that I have used religiously a couple of times a week, every week, for more than a decade. Not only have these exercises kept me virtually free from back pain, they have helped me train for triathlons. Having a strong core is vital for biking, swimming, and running. I probably could have found these exercises in books, but Jeff's one-on-one, personal help was invaluable. The credibility factor learning from Jeff was high. He has practiced these exercises and trained hundreds of others in doing them. He's also in incredible shape. The dude has participated in canoe races over a hundred miles long!

My hope is to be as effective as Jeff as I attempt to offer some "spirit-building exercises" that can greatly enhance your "spiritual core," your relationship with God. My conviction is that if one practices the spiritual disciplines, especially a daily, focused time of interacting with God, one's life will change dramatically. This conviction comes from my personal experience and from observing the lives of thousands of Christ followers I have known over the years. My hope is that out of these 101 spiritual exercises, you could find a dozen or so that you would use regularly because you sense your spirit growing stronger every time you practice these kinds of interactions with God. *"Physical training is good, but training in godliness is much better, promising benefits in this life and in the life to come"* (1 Timothy 4:8).

Some of these exercises will stretch you. That will be good for you if you are stuck in a routine of "daily devotions" that are no longer life-giving. Some will feel rather mystical; you might expect to hear Gregorian chant music in the background. Using your imagination will be mandatory for most. A few will seem rather "unspiritual" until you try them. Some will undoubtedly pull you out of your comfort zone. A quick look at the bibliography will show you that I draw from numerous streams of Christianity. So if you are from an Evangelical background you will be weirded out by a few. Catholic and Orthodox believers will also wade into some unfamiliar waters of Evangelicalism.

Every one of these exercises is designed to cultivate an authentic, robust spirituality that is rooted in Creator God's initiating, pro-active, kind, unconditional, fatherly, transforming love that is offered to us through Jesus Christ. My hope is that people who are not yet followers of Jesus will experience the uniqueness of His loving presence by exploring a broader, richer spirituality than they've ever known. True spirituality

But, most of us don't have a month to spend at a monastery. More realistic for many of us would be a weekend prayer retreat in which we try five to ten of these exercises. Exercise sixty-five suggests ways to plan such a prayer retreat, but don't wait for a prayer retreat. Carve out an hour this week to start.

You will notice that I give personal examples of what each exercise has meant for me. I wrestled with this because I don't want to give false impressions about my own spirituality. It will become obvious that I'm a fellow pilgrim on this spiritual adventure. I just like to run into a fellow traveler that's been on the trail I'm about to hike and ask him directly: "Hey, what's it like around that next bend?" [2]

Keep in mind the ultimate the goal: to position yourself to encounter God, not just mechanically run through all of the exercises. The end goal of these exercises is connection to a Person, not a religious performance or even a spiritual workout.

1

A PRAYER JOURNAL

We start with the prayer journal exercise because most of the other one hundred exercises in this book will be enhanced if you write out your thoughts, feelings, prayers, questions, and responses as you interact with God. It is beneficial to keep all of these in one place. Why not a prayer journal? I realize that a notebook and pen have fallen out of vogue for some. No worries. Use your favorite digital note-taking device. What's important is that you see journaling as a tool to serve you in connecting with God.

Maybe you have yet to see the value of keeping a prayer journal. Maybe you've tried it but failed to make it part of your lifestyle. Whatever the case, remember you're not a slave to your journal. Here's a simple way to start (again):

1. Look for a simple notebook that fits you. Don't spend a lot of money on one of those leather ones until you get into the daily discipline. Don't get the kind with the date at the top (otherwise you feel guilty looking back over those blank pages). I prefer books with lines. Other members of my family are artists so they choose journals with blank pages that allow them to be more creative.

2. Write out the date at the top of the entry. I add the location if I'm somewhere other than "home."

3. Now, imagine writing a letter to God (trust me, He is reading it). Tell Him what you are grateful for. Tell Him

how much you love Him. Tell Him how you feel. Tell Him what you want to experience through journaling out your prayers.

4. Now read it out loud to Him. Add whatever else flows from your stream of consciousness.

5. You may be reluctant to be completely honest about what you are recording (for fear that someone else may sneak a peek into your journal) but as you read it out loud as a prayer, you have the freedom to be completely honest.

6. Has this helped you communicate better with God? Try it every day for a week using some of the exercises in this book.

7. If you miss a day or two, just start over. The key to every spiritual discipline to not be consistent, but to be persistent. Have a dogged determination to keep starting over.

On a Personal Note

There are at least five benefits I've discovered in keeping a prayer journal:

1. I can track what God is teaching me through His Word and my life experiences. I listen better with my journal and pen in hand (I'll explain later the power of praying Scriptures—I can't imagine praying in this way without using a prayer journal).

2. I can always better articulate the inner places of my heart to God after I have expressed them on paper.

3. I have a record of the ways God has poured out His love on me day after day. To date there are tens of thousands of prayers of gratitude for His "good and perfect gifts" (James 1:17) in my life.

4. I have a record of some of my prayers… those answered and those yet to be answered. My faith is greatly built as I read over past prayer journals.

5. I can better communicate with Janine and my closest friends about the essence of my interaction with God. At the end of our personal prayer times Janine and I often share what we've recorded in our journals in order to more effectively and intimately pray for each other.

How often do I make an entry in my journal? For the first ten years of keeping a prayer journal, I recorded some of the things I was praying two or three times a week. For more than three decades now, journaling is a daily delight.

EXERCISES THAT CULTIVATE GRATITUDE

2

Count Your Blessings

Let your lives overflow with thanksgiving
for all that He has done…
(Colossians 2:7 NLT).

Being grateful is something that one *does*. Whether we feel grateful or not, we can "do gratitude" Here's one way to *overflow with gratitude*:

1. Make a list of all the ways you have been blessed in the last twenty-four hours. Give yourself time to reflect on what has happened. Make note of:

   - good news you heard from a friend
   - an email that encouraged you
   - a conversation that went really well
   - an answered prayer
   - something someone did for you that was kind or gracious
   - a positive emotion you experienced
   - a meal you really enjoyed
   - a dreaded task you put behind you
   - any other accomplishment
   - a gift
   - a pleasurable experience
   - something that made you laugh or smile
   - or 100+ other possible blessings

The items on your list do not have to be "spiritual." But you can interpret that experience as an expression of God's love for you. It doesn't have to be enormous or profound to be gratitude-worthy. Nothing is too small to evoke gratitude. Write down anything that comes to mind. It could be some inspiring thought you had or an insight that rocked your world. Or it could be a bowl of your favorite ice cream. Make it specific. Keep it recent. When you practice this daily you keep a sort of running tally of God's lavish gifts in your life.

When I make my list in my journal I put the symbol ✓ in front of each item which is code for "thank you Lord for. , , ," For example:

- ✓ the delightful meal we shared with Terry and Sue last night.
- ✓ healing me - how much clearer my sinuses feel this morning
- ✓ that funny YouTube video John sent me
- ✓ leading me to call Don and encourage him

2. After you have made your list, read it out loud as if you are talking directly with the One who is responsible for these gifts (James 1:17). Verbalize anything else that comes to mind.

   I have practiced this one daily for more than fourteen years. I see it as an offering to God that He delights in. *Through Him then, let us continually offer up a sacrifice of praise to God, that is, the fruit of lips that give thanks to His name* (Hebrews 13:15 NASB).

   As I do gratitude in this way:

   - I begin to feel more grateful than I did before.
   - I begin to be more aware of God's love for me.

- I begin to cultivate gratitude toward others.
- I am more obedient because I am told to "overflow with gratitude."
- The Lord is honored and blessed. (Read Luke 17:11-19 to see how Jesus appreciates gratitude).

On a Personal Note

I've been more consistent with this discipline than any of the following ninety-nine. I've actually done this exercise 360+ days a year for the last fourteen years. I'm not kidding! Nothing I can do more is more important than stopping long enough to tell God how much I appreciate Him. On a good day I will come up with twelve to fifteen items for which I am sincerely grateful. My guess is that there are probably at least one hundred more ways that God has shown me His love in the last twenty-four hours of which I am unaware. You can't go wrong cultivating a grateful heart!

3

Focused Gratitude

Every good thing I have comes from you
(Psalm 16:2b NLT).

In this exercise, rather than listing as many things as possible for which we *do* gratitude, we chose one for which we already have a sense of gratitude.

1. Think of **one thing you appreciate.** This can be something in nature, a baby's smile, a particular food, a person, a pet, a memory of a positive experience. . . anything that makes you feel real feelings of gratitude. It does not need to be something "spiritual," but simply anything that you genuinely appreciate.

2. Name it: Colorado, the Summer of 1999, Spot, gardenias, Beth, fall, the first norther, et cetera.

3. Focus your thoughts on that one thing and let positive feelings associated with that experience, place, memory, thing or person fill you mind and emotions. Savor it.

4. Express thanks to God for this amazing gift. Repeat your expression of gratitude until you begin to feel fresh waves of gratitude for God as the giver of every good and perfect gift in your life (James 1:17).

5. Tell someone else about your gratitude to God for this one particular gift.

On a Personal Note

I'm indebted to my friend Jim Walter for introducing me to this new way to grow in gratitude.[3] I find myself taking more time to put my life on pause and reflect on something that brings a smile to my face. Last night I took time to watch the moon come up over a mountain. I savored the moment and celebrated the fact that God cares so much for me that he *set the moon in place*, with people like me in mind (see Psalm 8:3-4). Talk about experiencing JOY!

4

TURNING STRESS INTO GRATITUDE

*Give thanks in all circumstances; for this is
God's will for you in Christ Jesus*
(1 Thessalonians 5:18).

For most of us, experiencing the negative emotions associated with stressful circumstances in our lives comes easier than gratitude. All kinds of circumstances can increase the stress level in our lives. There are daily stressors like a flat tire, losing one's cell phone, forgetting an important appointment, or having to face an unpleasant task. There are also long term stressful circumstances that take their toll on us emotionally and keep us from feeling grateful. Paul didn't say, "give thanks **for** all circumstances," but rather "**in** all circumstances." Some of our circumstances may not come from God but He can work through any on them for our good (Romans 8:28).

1. Name a specific cause of stress in your life right now (an immediate cause or a long-term cause).

2. Tell God how you feel about that particular circumstance. Be honest.

3. Now ask Him to help you do gratitude. "Father, I feel _____ *(frustrated, bitter, hopeless)* and I really want to give You thanks right now despite what's going on here. Please help me see something I can be grateful for."

31

4. Ask Him how He is redeeming this situation, how He wants to reveal Himself, and how He wants to make you more like Jesus.

5. Thank Him for whatever comes to mind.

6. If you are still struggling to be grateful for how God is working, go back to re-experience the gratitude for His good and perfect gifts you were aware of in the previous exercise.

On a Personal Note

Where I live, driving is very stressful. The roads are much too narrow for the number of cars and scooters vying for the right of way. I have to be very intentional to keep an attitude of gratitude when I drive. I often fail at this but I am learning to *drive in the Spirit* by practicing this discipline.

5

GRATITUDE FOR PEOPLE

I have not stopped giving thanks for you,
remembering you in my prayers (Ephesians 1:6).

It is obvious that the Apostle Paul was grateful for the people to whom he wrote. It was important for him to pray his gratitude. Here's one devotional exercise we can do that imitates the prayer life of this great apostle:

Think of the people in your life for whom you are most grateful. For many of us this list will be easy to create and could be quite lengthy. Start with someone with whom you are very close: a parent, spouse, sibling or child. Beside their name, list specific things about them for which you are grateful. For example:

Janine my precious wife, ✓ forty plus years of life with her as my best friend, ministry partner, lover, and co-parent ✓ she is smart, trustworthy, and loves You with all her heart ✓ her loyalty ✓ her courage ✓ she is an excellent mom and grandmother ✓ she is always putting other's needs above her own.

Verbalize what you have written and add other character traits and strengths that come to mind as you pray.

Proceed down your list identifying the things about each person you appreciate. Be specific and sincere. Express gratitude to God for who they are and the fact that God has brought them into your life.

Now think of someone who you want God to change. It might be easy to identify unhealthy or negative traits about this person. **Before** you plead with God to change them, thank God for their strengths, their positive character traits. Thank God for the way He is using them to work Christ's character in you!

Wouldn't it be great to receive an email today from someone you know that begins like: "As I was thinking about you today I felt such gratitude to God for you. Your kindness to me personally has often made me feel so special. . . ."

Practice praying this way first for whoever is on your prayer list today. Can you imagine the health in marriage relationships or between siblings or parents and their children if we prayed together expressing this kind of gratitude before God?

On a Personal Note

I don't do enough of this. "Lord please develop in me a habitual *gratitude first* prayer style. Please prompt me to express my gratitude more often in emails, text messages, and phone calls."

6

Join in the Blessings of Others

Rejoice with those who rejoice (Romans 12:15).

L ife is rich when we take the time to pause and celebrate God's goodness in our lives. We find even *more opportunities* when we learn to celebrate God's blessings in the lives of others. For example, I hear the news that a single woman whose parents I know well just got engaged to a godly man who seems like a perfect match. I can breathe a prayer of gratitude with a smile, thinking about God's grace to answer her prayers and the prayers of her parents and friends. I can cultivate my "spiritual radar" to be attentive to such blessings throughout my day. Here's a simple way we can obey this admonition:

1. Think about people in your family and Christian community who have been blessed lately: a new job, a baby, success on a new diet, good grades in school, a good report from a check-up, or any answer to prayer. Take time to tell God how happy you are for them. Praise Him for His grace in their lives.

2. Be particularly attentive to the blessings in others' lives that *you yourself have been asking for but have yet to experience.* We "spit in the eye" of jealousy or envy when we choose to celebrate God's grace on others when we ourselves are in a "not-yet-answered prayer" mode. We can truly be happy

for others even when we wish we were blessed in the same way. We really DO TRUST GOD when we can celebrate His goodness to others.

3. This simple command says: Rejoice **with** those who rejoice. How fitting to make a call or send an email or text message that says: "I am so happy for you. I celebrate the way God has blessed you with _____."

A way to apply this to a small group gathering or family devotions is as follows. Anytime someone shares God's work in their lives, a testimony of answered prayer, unexpected blessing, or one reason why they are happy, stop and rejoice with them!

On a Personal Note

My daily gratitude list increased dramatically when I began to reflect on what I could celebrate in the lives of others.

7

CREATING YOUR OWN PSALM
OF GRATITUDE

*None can compare with you; were I to speak and tell of
your deeds, they would be too many to declare*
(Psalm 40:5b).

Many of the Psalms are the lyrics of songs of gratitude
sung to God for the last twenty-eight centuries. It is
impossible to improve on these powerful, heartfelt, anointed
expressions of gratitude, but we can personalize them and even
create our own annotated paraphrased versions. Here's how:

1. Select one of the following Psalms: 18, 21, 30, 32, 40:1-
    11; 66:13-20; 92, 116, 118, 138.

2. Read it out loud slowly.

3. Now take each verse from the top and create a paraphrase
    version in your own words. You can write it out or just
    recreate the essence of the verse extemporaneously. If you
    write it, read what you have written out loud as a personal
    prayer. For example, take the above verse: "None can com-
    pare with you; were I to speak and tell of your deeds, they
    would be too many to declare" (Psalm 40:5b). My version
    would read: "No one comes close to being as awesome as
    you. If I were to try to recite all the ways you have shown
    your love to me in tangible, powerful ways, it would take
    more than a lifetime."

For example, my friend Peter Nevland has done this well. He has taken many of the Psalms and rewritten them with his own poetic flare. Check it out at: www.emusic.com/album/peter-nevland-co/...the-psalms/15871760

On a Personal Note

After practicing this approach to reading many of the Psalms I now do it automatically. Personalizing many of the statements of the Psalms helps me connect with God emotionally, especially through feeling grateful.

8

TURNING BIBLE READING
INTO PRAYERS OF GRATITUDE

Thanks be to God for His indescribable gift!
(2 Corinthians 9:15).

God is so worthy of our gratitude for the good gifts He is pouring out in our lives day-to-day and for the people He has brought into our lives. There are also "big picture" gifts such as the love relationship we enjoy with Him through the sacrificial death of Jesus Christ. Forgiveness of our sins, redemption, and the promise of eternity are real and tangible ways He has loved us, but they become more real to us when we vocalize our gratitude to Him for what He has done.

A simple exercise we can do to express our gratitude to Him is by turning what we read in the Bible into prayers of gratitude. One can find expressions of God's love for us on nearly every page of the Bible. Take any chapter and there's something we see about God, His character, His redemptive plan for us, His acts to establish His kingly reign in our world, and His personal, kind, fatherly, proactive love for us. All of these are praiseworthy.

Let's do this exercise with a straight-forward, easy to interpret, relatively short chapter of the New Testament: 1 John 1.

1. Read it slowly, out loud.

2. Now read the first verse again and tell God/Jesus what you appreciate about Him from this verse. For example: "Thank you Jesus that You existed from the beginning. Thank You that You became so human that people (like John) saw You, heard You, and touched You. *You made such an impression on them.* Wow. You *are* the Word of Life."

3. Now look for things that you love about God/Jesus in verse two. Continue to do the same in the following verses.

4. One benefit of a prayer journal would be to record your "thankful list" for posterity. Some Bible apps allow you to add personal notes.

5. If you write out your prayers of gratitude, it's meaningful to also verbalize these written prayers out loud to God.

Try this on one of the gospel narratives or a "dense" chapter in Paul's writings like Romans 8 or Ephesians 1. Ask the question, "What does this say about God?" Remember that Jesus is the "visible image of the invisible God" and remember how He has showed you His love. Turn that into an expression of heartfelt gratitude and see how much better you get to know Him.

On a Personal Note

The Word has become alive to me through this exercise. One day I read Luke 15 and understood it like never before (I'm sure I have read it at least 100 times before and even taught it on at least a dozen occasions). This is what became so real to me: these three stories are not primarily about lost sheep, coins or sons. These stories are Jesus' response to the criticism the religious people had of Him that He loved to hang out with sinners (see verses 1-2). Jesus was saying in each story, **"This is what God is really like."** We have the shepherd, the woman, and the father. Every time I read that chapter I stop and express my gratitude to God that He loves sinners and is actively seeking to "find" us and bring us "home." He is also a joy-filled God and loves to share His joy with His friends.

9

Thanking God for Health

Always giving thanks to God the Father for everything, in the name of our Lord Jesus Christ
(Ephesians 5:20).

1. Find a comfortable sitting position in a quiet room where you are alone.

2. Settle your thoughts for a few moments, allowing your breathing to slow down and your body to relax.

3. Without moving, and in the same quiet state, focus all your attention on your right foot. Thank God for that foot. Remember a time when you may have injured it and how it is now healthy and pain free. Thank God for healing. Thank God for protection. Thank God for all the things you get to do because you have a right foot.

4. Do the same with your left foot. Thank God that you can walk, run, and stand up. Thank God that you haven't had to live with a disability that would confine you to a wheel chair. Continue to move up your body your ankles, shins, calves, knees, thighs, et cetera. Thank God for all the things you can do because you have legs.

Take time to thank God for every part of your body up to the top of your head. Thank Him because:

"For you created my inmost being;
you knit me together in my mother's womb.
I praise you because I am fearfully and wonderfully made;
your works are wonderful,
I know that full well"
(Psalm 139:13-14 NIV).

Thank Him that you don't have cancer or some other horrendous disease.

What if you have a birth defect or an injury that has resulted in permanent damage to some part of your body? What if you are suffering from a disease? You can thank Him that it's not worse. You can thank Him because He is your healer. You can thank Him for the hope of a miracle. You can thank Him for how He has and will redeem what you have suffered. Thank him for the parts of your body that are healthy and function well. Thank Him for our future new bodies that will be perfectly whole.

On a Personal Note

I've never had a "body image" issue, but there are certainly things about my body I would really like to be different. I would love to have hair on top of my head! But when I choose to *do* gratitude for my physical appearance, I *feel* more content with the way God made me.

10

ONE THOUSAND GIFTS

And I pray that you will learn to give thanks to the father,
who has made you fit to share the inheritance of
God's holy ones in the light
(Colossians 1:12 The Kingdom New Testament).

Ann Vosskamp has inspired millions through her discovery of the power of gratitude and her brilliant way of communicating that discovery in her book: *One Thousand Gifts*.[4] As she sought to cultivate gratitude for even the simplest of life's pleasures, like mail in the mailbox, or moonlight on a pillow, her eyes were opened to the immenseness of God's blessings on her life. She has come to the conclusion that eucharisteo, Greek for "thanksgiving," is:

- the mystery to the fullest life;
- the source of truest, purest joy;
- the holy grail;
- inherent to a true salvation experience;
- the manifestation of our Yes to His to grace;
- the igniter of faith; and
- much, much more.

This exercise differs from the ones described above in that Ann kept a running list of new things for which she was grateful. Her goal was to reach one thousand. Her life was dramatically changed before she reached that goal. . . and the practice of noting God's variegated, multi-dimensional, profound gifts to us will transform our lives also.

To compile a list of one thousand things you are grateful for may take a year. You might start with one hundred and give yourself a month. Better yet, break it down to three a day and see how long you can go.

On a Personal Note

I had been working on gratitude for years before reading Ann Vosskamp's book, but I found in it fresh inspiration for this practice. Surprisingly, the "gifts" she observed in her life were totally different than the things I see as gifts in my life. I found myself saying repeatedly: "O yeah, I love that, too," which reminds me that there are still so many ways God is loving me that I still do not notice.

11

GOD'S PROVISION

*And my God will meet all your needs according
to the riches of His glory in Christ Jesus*
(Philippians 4:19 NIV).

God provides for us in many ways that we never even acknowledge. We don't stop and give Him thanks because
we've never even taken the time to reflect on His provision.
Often we are focused on the "needs" we have that are yet
unmet. This simple exercise will help open your eyes to what
God has already done for you.

1. How has God provided for you recently? Come up with a
   list of ten ways that God has fulfilled this promise in Philippians 4:19. To jumpstart your awareness, think about
   the obvious: the place you live, the vehicle you drive, your
   clothing, the food in your pantry and fridge, your furniture, TV, and others.

2. After you've come up with ten things, tell God how much
   you appreciate these things and all that He has provided
   for you.

3. Now, pray for someone you know who doesn't have what
   you've been given. Ask the Father: "Is there something
   someone else really needs that you would like to provide
   for them through me/us?"

4. Follow-through in obedience if something comes to mind.

On a Personal Note

I have lived thirteen years (so far) in a developing country. I have much more wealth than most of the people I know and interact with on a daily basis. It's so convicting to live among people who are far more content and thankful for so much less than we have owned throughout our lives. This exercise will train us for a new perspective.

12

THANKING GOD FOR HEARING US

This is the confidence we have in approaching God:
that if we ask anything according to His will, He hears us.
And if we know that He hears us—whatever we ask—
we know that we have what we asked of Him
(1 John 5:14-15).

For most of us, it's not a stretch to feel grateful to God for an answer to prayer and to express that to Him accordingly. What's much more challenging is to be grateful before we see the answer. To have such confidence in God that when we have prayed about something—to have poured our hearts before Him—to know that He has heard us—to have such confidence in Him shows that we truly believe He hears us.

Here's an exercise that can cultivate gratitude before we see what we have longed for.

1. Recall a request that you have brought before God repeatedly without a breakthrough. (Perhaps you've asked God for this thing for many years.)

2. From what you know from God's character and the Bible, does this thing you desire line up with God's will? Tell Him: "Father, as best as I understand Your will, I've asked for _____ in all sincerity."

3. Tell Him: "I believe your promises in...(quote or read: 1 John 5:14-15; Matthew 7:7; Mark 11:22-24)."

4. Now, using your imagination, envision what it will be like when this request is fulfilled. Play out the scene with as much detail as possible. Imagine how thrilled you will be and how grateful to God you will be.

5. Thank God as if that imagination has become a reality.

On a Personal Note

Many of us have seen this idea of faith abused. What keeps it healthy is to keep it real by being honest and accurate with others. For example, when telling others about my desire for a breakthrough, I don't "confess it" by making it sound like the answer to prayer has already come. Rather, I say, "I'm choosing to believe God's promise that He has heard me and the answer is on the way" or "I'm looking to Him for help" or "I am hopeful that God is hearing my prayers for this."

Secretly, alone with God, it can be a powerful faith-builder to rejoice before Him as if what we are asking for is on the way.

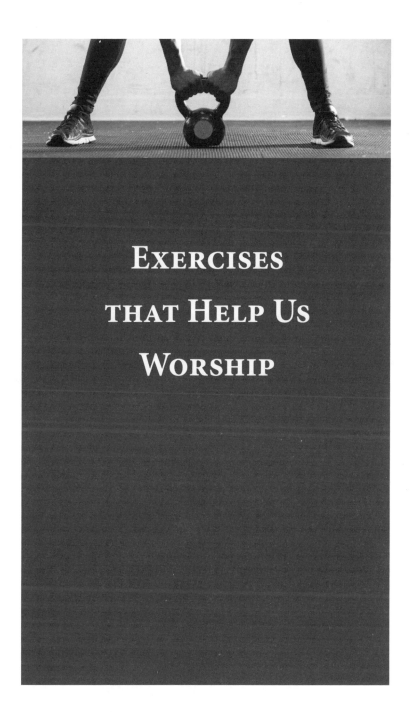

Exercises
that Help Us
Worship

13

AWESTRUCK BY THE SIZE OF GOD

The heavens declare the glory of God;
the skies proclaim the work of His hands
(Psalms 19:1 NLT).

Some of my most significant encounters with God have been out away from the city under a canopy of stars. It's easy to remember how BIG God is when we gaze up in the night sky. Even if you can't get out of town away from light pollution (and other kinds of pollution), one can be caught up in the greatness of God through the following exercise.

1. Go outdoors on a clear night. If this doesn't work for you check out YouTube videos of the universe. Three that I would recommend are: Gigapixels of Andromeda [4K], Immensity of the Universe or The Detailed Universe.

2. Allow yourself to be awestruck by the immensity of God in creating our universe. If you have good eyesight and the sky is perfectly clear, you can see at the most 4,500 stars. You will see part of our galaxy, the Milky Way. It actually has over 300 billion stars (our sun is an average sized star). Astronomers estimate that there are at least one hundred billion galaxies in the observable universe! The current estimate for the number of stars in our universe is 700 billion trillion! And the number of planets could be at

least 8 times that number. . . more than the sand particles on every beach on our planet!

3. Read Psalm 19:1-6.

4. Praise God that He is the One that spoke these stars and planets into existence. "I praise you that you created each of these 700 billion trillion stars and you gave each of them a name" (see Psalm 147:3).

"I praise you that what we see in the night sky is what you made with your fingers. You set all these stars, planets and their moons in place yet you think about us, and care for us" (see Psalm 8:3-5).

5. Pray what Christians have prayed for centuries: "Your unfailing love, O Lord, is as vast as the heavens" (Psalms 36:5).

"Open our eyes to behold thy gracious hand in all thy works; that, rejoicing in thy whole creation, we may learn to serve thee with gladness . . . ." — *The Book of Common Prayer*[5]

On a Personal Note

My first walk with God out under the stars was more than forty-five years ago! It's now a lifestyle for me to be drawn out of doors at night where there's a place to take a walk by myself with the Father. Words are inadequate to capture the closeness I've felt to God on some of those walks. I'm often struck by the fact that the creator and ruler of the cosmos that I'm gazing into would stoop to walk beside a tiny speck of a human.

14

THE NAMES OF GOD AND JESUS

*Build my altar wherever I cause my name to be remembered,
and I will come to you and bless you*
(Exodus 20:24).

Worship at its most basic level is to acknowledge who God is. One way to adore Him is to declare the names of God or Jesus in prayers of adoration. There are over a hundred names for God or Jesus. Each of His many names describes a different aspect of His many-faceted character. You can find yourself caught up in the presence of God as you focus on the person of Jesus who is the exact representation of God—the clearest, most profound picture of God.

Here's one way to do this:

1. Start with making a list of ten or so names of God found in the Old Testament. The internet has numerous websites that can help us find the names of God used in both Testaments.

You will find names like

Elohim: God—Creator, Mighty, and Strong

El Shaddai—God Almighty

Jehovah-Jireh—The Lord Who Provides

Jehovah-Shalom—The Lord Our Peace

2. With your list in hand, declare verbally to God who He is (no silent prayers here). "God, you are Jehovah-Jireh. You are *my* provider ..."

3. Now, make a list of names for Jesus: Shepherd, Author of Life, Lion of Judah, Light of the World, et cetera.

4. Now say the list of names back to Him in adoration. Feel free to expound on these declarations.

On a Personal Note

In the early 1980's I was inspired by Larry Lea who taught this principle in a book entitled *Could You Not Tarry One Hour.*[6] I prayed these Hebrew names for God and names used for our Savior nearly every morning for almost a decade. How often I experienced a significant increase in faith for a breakthrough as I declared God to be the God of the breakthrough before petitioning Him for the breakthrough!

15

THE ABC's OF ADORATION

Through Him then, let us continually offer up sacrifice of praise to God, that is, the fruit of lips that give thanks to His name.
(Hebrews 13:15 NASB).

M ost of us need help in expressing adoration to God. If you don't believe that, just try leading a prayer meeting in which the participants are asked, "Right now, let's just pray prayers of adoration." See what happens. People will almost immediately jump into petition prayers or other kinds of prayers that express needs or longings. Why? Because few Christians have the vocabulary of adoration. That muscle is under-developed. This exercise is designed to increase our core spiritual strength through expressions of praise to the One who is so worthy.

Start with the letter 'A' and think of as many words as you can to describe God. Here are some that are on my list: awesome, Abba, affirming, always, alive, abundant, accepting, able, active, absolute, abiding, amazing…. Then continue on to letter 'B' and do the same.

When I first developed this list I used a dictionary and a thesaurus as I worked through the alphabet. This was a profound devotional experience. My list has grown as I have come across new words to describe God and even new impressions (revelations) of what God is like. "Resplendent" is not part of my daily vocabulary but I now use it frequently when praying prayers of adoration.

When ready, you can pray your ABC list out loud. "God you are _____." At the end of these prayers of adoration and praise, I often say: "God, you are all these things and *much more!*"

On a Personal Note

I use this exercise in worshipping the Father in a myriad of ways. I set my mind on God this way as I swim or perform other mindless tasks throughout the day. Even at night when trying to go back to sleep, I start with letter 'A' and work my way through the alphabet. Rarely do I get to 'E' before I experience a significant sense of God's presence. I've practiced it when washing dishes, mowing the lawn, waiting in line, or stuck in traffic. I sense God's pleasure when I do it. I already have a long list of these traits and characteristics of God/Jesus, but new adjectives are still being added. (See Appendix A for an example). "Oh, the depth of the riches of the wisdom and knowledge of God. How unsearchable His judgments, and His paths beyond tracing out!" (Romans 11:33).

This works well in a family or small group community. Children get into it. New believers with a minimal education in rural parts of Indonesia get into it. Try it!

16

God, I have Found You to Be…

"Remember that you were slaves in Egypt and the LORD
your God redeemed you" (Deuteronomy 15:15).

One of the most profound shortcomings of the people of
God in the Old Testament was their tendency to forget
God's incredible acts on their behalf. They were repeatedly
exhorted to remember God's divine intervention in their lives
and in doing so they remembered HIM. They worshipped Him
as Victorious Deliverer when they remembered the exodus.
When God acted on their behalf they often named the place
where He "showed up," so as to remember what He had done.

In this exercise we take time to recount the ways God has
worked in our lives and in doing so we declare His character.
Here are a couple of examples of ways God has revealed Himself to me and how I express my adoration to Him because I
have experienced Him in these ways:

"God I have found You to be…

- **My counselor**—giving me all the wisdom I need for every
  decision I face today.

- **My warrior**. You not only fight on my behalf, You train
  me for battle.

- **My truth-speaker.** You always tell me just how it is, both exposing the lies I'm telling as well as the lies I'm hearing from the enemy.

- **My hope**—for meaning, purpose, and success.

- **My father**—a kind, compassionate, proactive, disciplining, generous, and transforming Father who loves me unconditionally.

- **My burden-bearer.** You delight in taking the things I'm carrying, the heavy things that are weighing on my heart.

Take some time to reflect. How did God come through for you in times of intense trials, sorrow, disappointment, anxiety, or pain? Maybe you can recall times of intense love or joy you've experienced in His presence. If you are a Christian, He has shown Himself to be your forgiver and your freedom. Create a list. You might come up with only five to ten things you can say about God's personal revelation of Himself to you, but that list will grow as you take time to remember His works in your life. Speak out the things that come to mind: "God I have found you to be... ." As you declare His reality that you have come to know through His work in your life, your affection for Him will grow.

On a Personal Note

Each of my declarations are tied to events in my life in which God showed Himself to be these things to me. They are revelations of Himself tied to an event or multiple events in which He came through for me in that particular way. In other words: I have experienced God as my healer, friend, burden-bearer, father, et cetera, and have specific memories associated with each of these declarations.

17

BEFORE THE THRONE

In a loud voice they were saying: "Worthy is the Lamb, who was slain, to receive power and wealth and wisdom and strength and honor and glory and praise!"
(Revelation 5:12).

Although there are various ways to interpret the Book of Revelation, there is one thing we all can agree on: *it is a call to worship!* The picture that the author, John, paints of the glorious day of the Lord evokes in us a sense of anticipation of Jesus finally receiving the honor and worship that He is due. The reality of that future day invites us to humble ourselves right now and worship Him. This exercise is great preparation, a rehearsal, for the *big* event.

1. Read Revelation chapters four and five out loud. If you are alone, read the chorus with louder volume. If you are doing this with others have everyone read these sections together.

2. Now put on the music of Michael W. Smith's "Angus Dei." Let it keep repeating as background worship music.

3. Read the two chapters again, pausing periodically and with eyes closed. Envision the rich details of this scene. Focus on the "One sitting on the throne." Put yourself in the crowd witnessing this event. Pretend you are among those declaring and singing the choruses.

4. Join the twenty-four elders as they "fall down and worship the Lamb."

5. Imagine the millions of angels. Imagine every creature on earth and under the sea. Imagine people from "every tribe and language and people and nation" *all* worshiping the Lamb with *all* their hearts. Join them in declaring **His** worth!

On a Personal Note

The first time I did this I was with a group of missionaries from at least twenty different countries gathered for a retreat. We experienced a tangible sense of God's presence. Tears come to my eyes just recalling the revelation, in that moment, of how worthy Jesus is of this kind of honor. It was with great significance to that group when we reached the "every tribe and language and people and nation" part. All of us could name tribes, language, peoples, and nations that we anticipated being there. It was not a quiet, contemplative moment by any means. It was loud, intense and full of shouts intermingled with joyful weeping.

18

A LOVE LETTER

How do I love thee? Let me count the ways.
I love thee to the depth and breadth and height ...
— Elizabeth Barret Browning, *Sonnet 43*

Our words may never come close to the literary beauty of an Elizabeth Barret Browning poem, but taking time to tell God the things you love about Him in all the sincerity and depth of expression you can muster is something God treasures.

Early in my years of keeping a prayer journal, I found that imagining myself writing a love letter to God, with pen in hand, helped my words of adoration flow freely—unedited and unfiltered. I am embarrassed to offer an example, because I am poetically challenged but I believe God feels about my love letters the way Robert Browning must have felt reading Elizabeth's famous *Sonnet 43* written to him before they were married. In another earthly example, the more I know about being a father, the more I can imagine how our heavenly Father responds to our efforts just as I treasure the "blessings" that my children write in their cards to me.

This one is easy. Get something to write with (or use your laptop) and get going. Start with something like: "Jesus, what I love about you is…" After a paragraph or a page, read what you have written to Him as a prayer.

On a Personal Note

I view my prayer journals as a collection of my "love letters" to God. He is so worthy of our every expression of our love and gratitude. Recently, one of my daughters took time every day of Advent to tell Jesus one thing she loved about Him that she hadn't expressed the previous days. It was very rich!

19

A Love Song

Have you ever been singing along to a song that no one would ever sing in church (one of those "secular" tunes) and find yourself directing the words to Jesus? There are some really great lyrics out there, written with a natural lover in mind, that could be said of our Lord. Here are some lines of a couple of songs that I have turned into worship songs to the Lover of my soul.

"For all those times you stood by me
For all the truth that you made me see
For all the joy you brought to my life
For all the wrong that you made right

For every dream you made come true
For all the love I found in you."

—"Because You Loved Me,"
written by Diane Warren and sung by Celine Dion 1996

Now I'll be bold
As well as strong
And use my head alongside my heart
So take my flesh
And fix my eyes
A tethered mind free from the lies

And I'll kneel down
Wait for now
I'll kneel down
Know my ground.

—"I Will Wait for You"
by Mumford and Sons, 2012

This is how to go about it:

1. Look up your favorite love songs.
2. Find several that have words you can redirect upwards (to God).
3. You may want (or need) to change the lyrics of a line or two. Have fun with this.
4. Sing them with gusto.

If this feels unspiritual to you, remember that some of the most popular hymns written in the 18th and 19th Centuries were set to secular music that had been played in taverns!

On a Personal Note

Apparently, I'm not the only one who shamelessly co-opts popular tunes and changes the lyrics into a song directed to our Lord. As I've shared this habit with friends more than one has laughed and said: "I've done that for years."

20

Dancing Before
the Lord

*Let them praise His name with dancing
and make music to Him with timbrel and harp*
(Psalm 149:3).

This expression of worship is a stretch for many Christians.
Some church-goers see dancing as irreverent. Others
believe it is acceptable, yet personally feel uncomfortable or
awkward involving their limbs in worship. I can relate. It was
challenging for me to become free to dance in church even
though I am accustomed to exuberant worship.

Try this when you are home alone. Find some of your
favorite worship music that has a strong beat. Turn it up and
move your body. If you feel self-conscious, just be assured that
it is normal to feel that way. That's why it is best to make sure
no one is watching except God.

If you need to be convinced about the validity of this kind
of worship just look up "dance" or "dancing" in your Bible
concordance. We are admonished to dance. It's an obedience
issue. If you feel that dancing before God might be too weird,
read carefully the story of David welcoming the Ark which
represented God's presence (2 Samuel 6:16-22). David seems
to be doing more than just clapping his hands or swaying his
body. His was probably exuberant, uncontrolled flailing. You

get the impression God was more than okay with this form of praise.

Parents, disciple your children in dancing as a form of worship. They will love it. If they are still young, they will be much less inhibited than we are. Maybe this is what Jesus had in mind when He said we must become like children to enter His kingdom!

On a Personal Note

I was a Christian for twenty years before I found delight in letting my feet join my worship. It started with a simple hop and evolved into out-in-out flailing. Talk about freedom! I love to find settings where lovers of Jesus are going for it with abandoned worship that includes dancing. However, I'm still a bit self-conscious because of my uncoordinated style. But when no one's around, watch out furniture!

21

WORSHIP WITH INSTRUMENTS

Praise Him with the sounding of the trumpet,
praise Him with the harp and lyre,
praise Him with timbrel and dancing,
praise Him with the strings and pipe,
praise Him with the clash of cymbals,
praise Him with resounding cymbals
(Psalm 150:3-5).

This exercise seems fairly straight forward if you happen to play a musical instrument. Obviously people who play the guitar or piano have an advantage, but any instrument can be played as worship to God. Whatever your skill level, you can play as unto God. He appreciates our efforts even if we lack talent.

Non-musicians can take heart. Any number of objects can be used to make a "joyful noise" to the Lord (1 Chronicles 15:16). Years ago my wife Janine was asked to speak at a women's gathering in a village in the mountains of Central Java, Indonesia. As part of their worship experience, a group of women from a church in a neighboring village led out in a song they had prepared using kitchen utensils. Spoons, pots, pans, cups, and glasses were used to make music to God. Tears streamed down their tan, weathered cheeks as these women presented their offering of adoration to God. Imagine how beautiful it sounded to Him!

Try it. Play along with your favorite worship music on a homemade instrument. Or turn off your stereo or smart phone and create your own sound. Use kitchen utensils or whatever you can find to create a joyful noise. Almost anything can be turned into a drum.

On a Personal Note

I've always been a bit envious of people with musical talent. Singing and playing musical instruments seems to come easier for everyone else in my family than it does to me. One day, I was lamenting before the Lord about my inability to sing and I sensed the Lord say: "I love your voice." "I delight in your songs of praise to Me." That's all that really matters, that God loves our voices and musical talent.

22

BORROWING FROM THE PRAYERS OF OTHERS

May God the Father who made us bless us.
May God the Son send His healing among us.
May God the Holy Spirit move within us and give us,
Eyes to see with, ears to hear with,
and hands that your work might be done.
May we walk and preach the word of God to all.
May the angel of peace watch over us and lead us,
At last by God's grace to the Kingdom
(from St. Dominic 1170-1221).

There are many time-tested prayers prayed by others who lived in centuries past. Check out the power and life in St Dominic's prayer quoted above. There are people who are more articulate than us and who have ways of praying from which we have much to learn.

1. Find one of the following sources (many of these are available on-line without having to purchase them):
   • *The Divine Hours* by Phyllis Tickle
   • *The Book of Common Prayer*
   • *Celtic Prayers from Iona* by J. Philip Newell
   • *Celtic Daily Prayer for ALL Who Seek God* by Norman Shawchuck and Ruben P. Job

- *Devotional Classics: Selected Readings for Individuals and Groups* by Richard J. Foster
- *The Ignatian Adventure: Experiencing the Spiritual Exercises of St. Ignatius in Daily Life* by Father Kevin O'Brien SJ

2. Read through one of these classics until you find a prayer that resonates with the cry of your heart. Read it out loud as unto God.

3. There are also more contemporary prayer guides that jump-start our own prayers. My friend Steve Hawthorn has created a powerful prayer guide called *Seek God for the City* that leads us through 30 days of prayer leading up to Easter every year.[7]

4. Don't expect to connect with all of the prayers that you find. You may have to read through a dozen of them until you find one that expresses your personal longings. If one of the above resources doesn't connect for you, try another.

On a Personal Note

I use these kinds of borrowed prayers rarely and in small doses. Many of them are far more poetic and articulate than I could ever be, but I find it challenging to make them *my prayers*. I may be wrong, but I picture God being like me when it comes to expressions of love = from family and friends. A *Hallmark* card says it well, but a personal note means so much more. Having said this, I recently read The Ignatian Adventure: *Experiencing the Spiritual Exercises of St. Ignatius in Daily Life* by Father Kevin O'Brien SJ. I could hardly put it down. I was amazed at how much I connected with St. Ignatius.

23

SHOUT OUT YOUR PRAISE

Come, let us sing for joy to the LORD; let us shout
aloud to the Rock of our salvation
(Psalm 95:1).

The word shout is found 159 times in both Testaments of the Bible. Most of those shouts are shouts of praise to God. It's interesting how awkward it is for many Christians, people who will scream their lungs out at a football game, to shout praise to God. As worshippers, we become rather timid. Yet in the Psalms, shouting seems as common as singing in the context of worship. It is so liberating to become vocal, even loudly so, in worship.

Here are a couple of ways you can get loud in your expression of love to God:

1. If your church is not into shouting, find a large charismatic or Pentecostal church or worship gathering where you won't stand out if you shout. Often churches of certain ethnic groups are much more free in their vocal expressions. Find one, slip in the back and go for it.

2. On your commute to work, alone in your car, crank up some worship music, then shout it out: "God you are awesome," "Way to go God, "You are my victorious warrior," et cetera. Obviously, other places where you are completely alone are good places to start.

3. If you are a worship leader in a church or leading your family or small group in a time of worship, convince them to join you in a cheer of unison. It is such fun!

I know some will say: "What if I don't feel like shouting?" That is the best time to shout! It's an even better time to shout if you feel discouraged or defeated. Choosing to shout out victorious praise to God is just what you need for your heart to come alive in God. A Vineyard song written by Kevin Prosch says it well: *Shout to the Lord, shout to the Lord, shout to the Lord of Hosts And it breaks the heavy yoke, breaks the heavy yoke.*

On a Personal Note

What I'm suggesting here, I have done on many occasions. This is not natural for me, but the more I've grown in love with God, the more I feel free to express that love, even in shouting.

24

PRAISING GOD FOR WHAT HE HAS MADE

How many are your works, LORD!
In wisdom you made them all;
the earth is full of your creatures
(Psalm 104:24).

God must have had people like me in mind when He inspired the writing of Psalm 104. It is a poem and worship song for people who are inspired to worship when they are out in nature or watching nature videos. If you read it carefully, you will notice that one of the themes of this Psalm is the flora and fauna of the earth. Even the creatures of the sea were designed by our creator *for Him and us* to enjoy. God delights in what He has made. So should we.

Here are a couple of simple ways we can delight in what He has made:

1. Find a meadow, or wooded area, or even a city park with a lot of trees. Take a walk with the specific purpose of observing every plant, animal, and insect you can find. Look carefully at the design of the leaves. Admire the flowers. Listen carefully to the sounds the birds make. Let the rustling of the leaves become praise to God. Note every detail.

2. Read Psalm 104 out loud. Personalize it as much as possible.

3. Tell God how much you appreciate His creativity, His humor, His workmanship, His love for beauty. Tell Him how much you delight in creation.

4. If you are housebound or are trapped in an urban jungle, watch a good nature program. It's hard to beat Planet Earth or Nature on PBS.

5. Sing one of these ancient hymns: "I Sing the Mighty Power of God," "This Is My Father's World," "Great Is Thy Faithfulness," or "Joyful, Joyful We Adore Thee." I love the YouTube worship video with Brian Doerksen's "Creation Calls" at https://youtu.be/lnNIp1Q4wsM.

6. Make it a worship experience by telling God how much you appreciate what you are seeing. A prayer found in the Book of Common Prayer says it well: "Open our eyes to behold *thy* gracious hand in all *thy* works; that, rejoicing in *thy* whole creation, we may learn to serve *thee* with gladness. . . ."

On a Personal Note

I connect with God so much easier when outdoors. It makes sense if you think of meeting the artist in his art gallery with his work on display. I recently came across a poem by Mary Oliver entitled "Messenger." A couple of lines capture the reason why I love to pray outdoors: "My work is loving the world. Here the sunflowers, There the hummingbirds—equal seekers of sweetness. . . . Am I no longer young, and still not half-perfect? Let me keep my mind on what matters, which is mostly standing still and learning to be astonished."

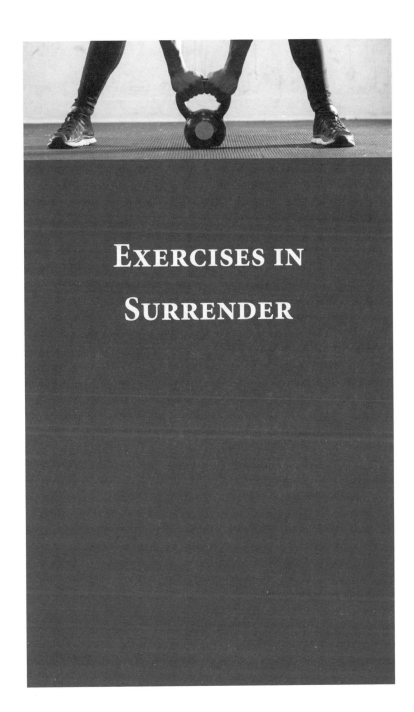

EXERCISES IN

SURRENDER

25

Our Bodies—His Temple

*Do you not know that your bodies are temples of the Holy
Spirit, who is in you, whom you have received from God? You
are not your own; you were bought at a price.
Therefore, honor God with your bodies*
(1 Corinthians 6:19-20).

*… offer every part of yourself to Him as an
instrument of righteousness*
(Romans 6:13).

1. Find a comfortable sitting position in a room where you
   are alone and which is quiet.

2. Settle your thoughts for a few moments, allowing your
   breathing to slow down and your body to relax.

3. Without moving and in the same quiet state, focus all your
   attention on your feet. Pray consecration prayers: "Lord,
   these feet are yours." "Come, Spirit of God." "Live in your
   temple." "May these feet carry me wherever you want me
   to go."

4. You can work your way up through your body: your legs,
   your torso, your arms, your head, brain, eyes, your tongue,
   even your internal organs. Offer them as instruments of
   righteousness. The context of the above verses would em-
   phasize our need to acknowledge that even our sex organs
   part of God's temple.

5. Declare that this body is *all* His. Repent of ways that your body has not been fully given over to God.

6. Commit every part of your body to come in line with the reality that it is God's temple.

7. Envision your whole body being filled with God's Spirit, bringing Him great honor and glory.

Therefore, I urge you, brothers and sisters, in view of God's mercy, to offer your bodies as a living sacrifice, holy and pleasing to God—this is your true and proper worship (Romans 12:1).

On a Personal Note

I like to combine Exercise Nine "Thanking God for Your Healthy Body" and this one. As I start with my feet I both praise him for my healthy feet and all the things I've been able to do with them, and then I offer them to God as instruments of righteousness (Romans 6:13).

26

OFFER PHYSICAL ASSETS TO GOD

In the same way, those of you who do not give up everything you have cannot be my disciples
(Luke 14:33).

To call Jesus "Lord" means He is in charge. He has full ownership of every aspect of our lives. Everything we would call "ours" is actually *His* if we follow Him. We are actually managers and not the owners of all the stuff He has entrusted to us.

1. Make a list of everything you "own." Write down your house(s), land, automobile(s), bike(s), boats, jewelry, furniture, lawn equipment, pets, appliances, dishes, clothing (you don't need to list every item), and keepsakes: *everything* you can think of. For most Americans, this list can be quite lengthy.

2. Now, list your financial assets. Write down the money in your checking and savings, accounts, stocks, bonds, retirement investments: *everything* you can think of.

3. Now start with the things that come to mind that seem most valuable to you. Imagine yourself bringing it to Jesus and laying it at His feet. Pray: "Lord Jesus, I love you and I want to acknowledge that this _____ is *not* mine, but yours. You have rightful ownership of _____." Or, "Following

you is *much more* important to me than me considering this _____ as my own."

4. If it helps, as you pray, open up the grip of your hands and release the item or the money into His hand or drop it at His feet. It helps me to imagine my financial assets being transferred to His account.

5. Ask: "Lord, is there someone, or a ministry that you want me to pass this asset on to?" If you can't pray this prayer with all sincerity, then you still consider yourself the owner.

6. For items or money that you don't sense you are to give away, reaffirm *His ownership* of with all of your heart. Express your willingness to always consider "your stuff" as HIS. Thank Him that He has entrusted so much to you for you to manage. Ask for His wisdom in your stewardship.

On a Personal Note

I was going down my list of assets one day, offering them to the Lord as the true owner of all that we considered "ours." I sensed the Lord speaking to me to give our house away. (Technically we owned only about 65 percent of the house when what we owed on the house was subtracted from the market value.) "You said it was mine, and that you are merely managers, right?" is what I sensed the Lord saying when I began to think sensibly about such a radical decision. There was no heaviness or sorrow in my heart. Only intense joy at the prospect of giving away our house. However, it took me a couple of weeks to work up the courage to share my impression with Janine. And it took her a couple of months to experience the grace to join me in this act of generosity. Our children were brought into the process and whole-heartedly agreed with our decision. The sacrifice was very real for us but in one sense it wasn't hard when we kept remembering that the house wasn't really ours. The moral of the story: God may take you up on your *offering*.

27

OFFER INTANGIBLE ASSETS TO GOD

… offer yourselves to God as those who have been brought from death to life; and offer every part of yourself to Him as an instrument of righteousness
(Romans 6:13).

This exercise mirrors the preceding one. The process is the same, but this time make a list of the intangibles: the talents, spiritual gifts, the personality God has given you, the dreams and longings of your heart, your career, your education, your family, your other relationships. Think about the rights you consider yours. What are the things about you that others admire or envy? Artistic abilities? Athletic abilities? List your strengths, reputation and influence.

Now, one by one, offer these parts of your life to God. Ask, "God is there something in my life that I have not fully entrusted to you?" "Is there something I'm not relinquishing to your authority?" With this kind of prayer, we are inviting God's kingly reign in every aspect of our lives.

On a Personal Note:

There are seasons during which we have wondered: "God are you really hearing this prayer of surrender? You seem to be wasting a lot of talent here." We so want God to use us for His glory but it seems He has us on the sidelines. The longer

I have known the Father the more I know that I know that He never wastes a life fully surrendered to Him. Periods of inactivity are times when He wants us to rest end enjoy Him more. Doors of fruitful ministry eventually open up and we forget that we were once not so busy. The key is to re-up on the surrender part and trust Him to let us know if there is something we are considering to be our rightful possession that is not-- something we need to transfer to His account.

28

OBEDIENCE-BASED
DISCIPLESHIP

*Jesus replied, "Anyone who loves me will obey my teaching.
My Father will love them, and we will come to them
and make our home with them"*
(John 14:33).

Many Christians equate spiritual maturity with biblical knowledge. We think if we know more of the Bible, we will automatically grow closer to God. Our attitude is: "Give me another insight, or inspiring thought, so I can live the Christian life." Many Evangelical Christians have become disillusioned with the Christian life as they have done their best to live out a set of Christian principles as if it were some kind of formula for success as a Christian. But from heaven's perspective, it is much more important that we love Him by obeying Him. We could bring the Kingdom to this present evil age if we simply walked in the light of the knowledge that we have. The following exercise is a way to read the Bible with a goal of living out what we are discovering about following Him.

1. Select any passage from the life, ministry, or teaching of Jesus. To start with, choose one that is no more than a dozen verses to start with.

2. Read it twice. Now retell it in your own words.
3. What does the passage say about Jesus (or the Father)?
4. What do we learn about people (like us) from this passage?
5. What is a command to obey or a pattern to follow from this passage?
6. Think about what you do within the week to begin to live out this command?
7. Pray a prayer: 1) Asking God's help, and 2) Committing to follow through with His help.

On a Personal Note

These questions are used in discipleship gatherings all over the world. I have been impressed by the life-transformation that happens in us when we read the Scripture with a mindset of obedience. This exercise is much more powerful when done in community. The Spirit seems to speak more clearly when we are together with others examining the Word this way. It is also much more helpful to be accountable to others. Finally, a good facilitator will help each of us *hear for ourselves* exactly what the Holy Spirit is telling us to do.

Exercises that Free us from Guilt and Shame

29

FORGIVEN

*Then God made you alive with Christ, for He forgave all our
sins. He canceled the record of charges against us
and took it away by nailing it to the cross*
(Colossians 2:13-14).

This exercise is particularly helpful if you find yourself
struggling with past failures or sins. Even if you are confident in God's forgiveness, it is good to pause and celebrate the
incredible grace of God that has freed us from all condemnation because of Christ's death on the cross.

Most of us who have read the Bible or sat through a number
of sermons know in our heads that we are (or can be) forgiven.
Our sins are so forgiven that God has forgotten them! But
sometimes our hearts bear the weight of shame from our past.
Here's one way to celebrate God's forgiveness.

1. If you don't happen to have a wooden cross in your home,
   yard or garage, make one. It can be simple and small. Use
   discarded lumber if that's all you have. If nothing else use
   a tree. Get a hammer and a nail.

2. Now, take a piece of paper and a pen. Write out every past
   failure that comes to mind. Begin with the ones that keep
   popping up in condemning thoughts. It could be sinful
   choices or actions that wrong God or others. Write out sinful attitudes you've harbored. Anything that is not keeping
   with God's character: evil habits and vile thoughts you have

allowed to take up residence in your heart like pride, gluttony, greed, envy or lust. The more recent failures you've struggled with are more significant to acknowledge than the ones you've been victorious over for years. If there is still any shame associated with these past failures, it's very important to write these down.

3. It is *not* necessary for you to mourn or grieve over these sins if you have confessed them and repented of them. We are celebrating what God has done if the Holy Spirit has already done His job of conviction and you have responded.

4. Now ask the Holy Spirit if He would point out anything you've not acknowledged or confessed. Pray *"Search me O God, and know my heart. . ."* (Psalm 139:23-24). *Ask Him to point out anything in your life that offends Him*

5. Take your list and nail it to the cross.

   Read the verse out of Colossians referenced above. Personalize it: *I praise you God that "You forgave all MY sins. You canceled the record of charges against ME and took it away by nailing it to the cross. As far as east is from west, You have removed our sin from us."*

6. In one more symbolic act, take your list down from the cross and burn it.

7. Now celebrate your forgiveness in Christ!

On a Personal Note

I found this exercise so meaningful for me personally that I made a cross for our church to participate. We have done it for many Good Friday worship gatherings. That same cross now resides in the prayer room. Thousands of sins written on small pieces of paper have been nailed to it with the knowledge that the original cross where Jesus died was the place of that once-for-all sacrifice that purchased our forgiveness.

30

A CLEAN SLATE

Let us draw near to God with a sincere heart and with the
full assurance that faith brings, having our hearts sprinkled to
cleanse us from a guilty conscience
(Hebrews 10:22).

This exercise helps us remember the sacrificial death of Christ and celebrate the cleansing His blood has brought to us.

1. Find a whiteboard that is at least two feet wide and two feet tall. You will also need an erasable marker (make sure they are not permanent markers) and an eraser.

2. Pull out a Bible (or your Bible App) and read carefully Hebrews chapters 9 and 10. Circle or highlight the words: "cleanse," "blood," "sacrifice," "atone" or "atonement." Read the verses out loud that contain these words.

3. At the top of the white board, write out one of your favorite verses from what you highlighted.

4. Now write: "The sacrificial death of Jesus has cleansed me from…"

5. List every sin you've committed that you can remember (I had to write really small). Include sins of the heart and sinful attitudes. Don't forget deliberate acts of disobedience and sins of omission (things you should have done but did not).

6. If time permits, watch Mel Gibson's The Passion of the Christ or the crucifixion scene from The Jesus Film. YouTube has numerous 4-6 minute versions of the passion set to worship music. Choose one that has a song you like.

7. Now reread the passages from Hebrews 9 and 10 that speak of Christ's sacrificial death for our sins.

8. Now erase every sin that you've acknowledged on that white board.

9. Take time and thank Him and worship Him for His cleansing and forgiveness. Thank Him for a clean conscience. Thank Him for cleansing of sins you've forgotten about or never even knew were in your heart. Thank Him for making you holy.

10. If you are doing this with your Christian community, it would be powerful to end this time by sharing the Lord's Supper together.

On a Personal Note

I often use the whiteboard illustration when sharing the gospel.

31

SILENCING THE LIES

*So now there is no condemnation for those
who belong to Christ Jesus*
(Romans 8:1).

I've never met a Christian that doesn't occasionally (and for some, often) have condemning thoughts like: "You are such a loser," "You will never succeed at anything," "You always lie," "You are such a hypocrite," or "You don't deserve being called a Christian." You know it is condemnation and not conviction when the "voice" is attacking your person or character (as opposed to the individual action). If it makes you feel worthless and condemned, the voice is *not* God. God's conviction is always directed at specific actions or attitudes and His voice calls us to repentance and freedom. Identifying the condemning lies that have been floating around in our heads is a major step toward a victorious heart. Here's a way to do this:

1. Find a comfortable sitting position in a room that is quiet and where you are alone.

2. Settle your thoughts for a few moments, allowing your breathing to slow down and your body to relax.

3. Think about negative thoughts that have been streaming through your head recently. Most of us can readily identify thoughts that have condemned us.

4. If nothing comes to mind, ask the Lord, "What are the condemning lies I've been believing lately?" Wait on the Holy Spirit.

5. When you have identified one, write it down or say it out loud.

6. Now ask, "What do you say about that Lord?" For example, you might be hearing: "You are such a loser." But the truth of God is: "I am more than a conqueror through Him who loves me," and "I can do all things through Christ who gives me strength." Declare the **truth**.

7. An alternative action when you have identified a lie is to laugh at or mock it. "So I'm hearing that I'm loser...ha! Nothing is farther from the truth. God says I can do all things through Him who gives me strength."

8. This is one of those exercises that's even more powerful with your trusted Christian community. When you are courageous and transparent enough to share with others those condemning lies, it will be very meaningful to allow them to help you speak the truth to those lies.

On a Personal Note

I once did this with a group of friends in our Christian community. We wrote on big note cards the lie or lies we had been hearing and then we turned the cards over to reveal what God says about us to counter the enemy's lies. What was amazing was that people who were incredibly smart were hearing how stupid they were. Beautiful people were hearing how ugly they were. People who sincerely love God were hearing what spiritual losers they were. Major freedom and incredible joy broke out among us when we identified the lies and declared God's truth.

32

ADDRESSING HURTFUL MEMORIES

Often a condemning lie in our subconscious comes from a painful experience from our past. For example, one day "out of the blue" I kept hearing: "You will never amount to nothing." It seemed so random, especially for a guy who has a pretty strong sense of confidence about most challenges in life. I practiced countering that lie with God's truth but it kept returning. The Holy Spirit then showed me when that lie lodged in my heart. My grandfather said it to me one day at the breakfast table when I was about six years old. In anger and frustration, he said: "Ronnie, you'll never amount to nothing." I had put this "curse" out of my memory, so I thought. But it must have wounded my young heart because that statement was set on "repeat" in my thoughts. I never realized its impact that I felt subconsciously until it emerged years later. Here is what I have learned we can do to address these painful memories:

1. In the previous exercise, if you readily identified a condemning thought that has repeatedly streamed through your consciousness over years, it's probably empowered by a painful experience from your childhood. Ask the Holy Spirit to take you back to that experience (you may need an experienced prayer counselor to walk you through this process).

2. Allow the Holy Spirit to help you remember the event, along with any sad or painful emotions you experienced in the moment. As I recounted that condemning statement from my grandfather, I remember feeling the blow to my heart. It was even more painful than if he had slapped me with his hand with great force.

3. Express the grief over the injustice of it all. For me, a six-year-old didn't need to hear that from an authority figure. Not only was it not true, it was also cruel and mean. Allow your heart to mourn the loss you experienced when painful words were spoken over you.

4. Ask, "Jesus, what would you say to me in this painful memory?" He might speak in any number of ways. Through our imagination Jesus may show how angry He was with the perpetrator. He might help you envision His comfort or protection. In my case, I sensed the Lord saying things like, "That's a *lie*," "He doesn't know what he's talking about," and "I have great plans for you." God then showed me how hurt and wounded my grandfather was in that moment. He was miserable because he was already feeling the effects of the cancer from which he eventually died. [For a thorough explanation of how God can meet you in imaginative prayer read Greg Boyd's *Seeing is Believing; Experiencing Jesus Through Imaginative Prayer.* [8]] Through this exercise of inviting the Lord to show up and speak into this painful memory, the lie that "Ron, you will never amount to nothing" was broken.

5. Ask the Lord help you forgive whoever inflicted pain on you.

6. Now speak out your forgiveness even if the person is not present or has passed away. "_____, I forgive you and release you to the One who judges justly and shows mercy."

7. If they are alive, pray a blessing on their life.

On a Personal Note

After practicing this exercise in response to the painful memory of my grandfather's hurtful words, the power of that condemning thought was broken. I have zero emotion connected with retelling the story other than pity for my grandfather.

EXERCISES THAT HELP US EXPERIENCE GOD'S LOVE

33

EXPERIENCING GOD'S LOVE THROUGH THE CROSS

*But God showed His great love for us by sending Christ to die
for us while we were still sinners*
(Romans 5:8 NLT).

A critical turning point in the life of Count Nicolas Ludwig von Zinzendorf was when he had a revelation of God's love for him through the suffering of Jesus Christ. It took place at an art gallery in Dusseldorf when he became transfixed with a painting of Christ wearing the crown of thorns in Dominico Feti's work *Ecce Homo*: "Behold, the Man!" He was overwhelmed with the love he saw in the face of Christ that the artist had drawn. It was a supernatural encounter that shaped his life. If Christ had loved him in this way, Zinzendorf thought, could he not give himself to the One who had captured his heart? Then and there he asked the slaughtered Lamb to draw him into "the fellowship of His suffering."[9]

Meditating on the suffering of Jesus seems rather morbid (or at least medieval) for modern Protestant/Evangelical Christians. But the cross is the most dramatic and powerful visible demonstration of God's love for us. It is imperative that we grasp this in order to truly experience God's love. The following exercise can position us to experience God's love demonstrated through the death of the Son of God, "who loved me and gave himself for me" (Galatians 2:20).

1. Rent, buy, or download a copy of Mel Gibson's *The Passion of the Christ.*

2. Pray in your own words something like: "Father, as I watch this depiction of the crucifixion of your Son Jesus, please give me a fresh revelation of the fact that He died for me."

3. Pause periodically throughout the film and read from the following list of verses:

   - Romans 5:6-9
   - Revelations 5:9
   - Mark 10:45
   - Romans 5:23-25
   - Hebrews 9:14, 26-28
   - Hebrews 10:19-20
   - 1 John 4:10-12
   - Ephesians 5:2
   - Galatians 2:20

4. After you read each verse, turn what you've read and watched in the film into prayers of gratitude.

5. At the end of the film, close with a time of worship, praying prayers of adoration.

On a Personal Note

I was recently speaking at Perspectives, a course on world missions, in Surabaya, Indonesia. I shared my part and was sitting in the back not really paying attention to the next speaker. Instead, I was involved in a conversation with a friend. While we were talking, a video clip from *The Passion of the Christ* started playing on the screen in front with the worship song "Thank You for the Cross" playing in the background. I lost it. The conversation had to pause while I wept. It was embarrassing. It was if I were hearing the story for the first time. The tears were flowing from a heart once again overwhelmed by the fact that Christ did it for me. May I ever see the cross as the ultimate expression of God's love.

35

BATHED IN AN OCEAN
OF GOD'S LOVE

"The Holy Spirit descended upon me in as manner that
seemed to go through me, body and soul. I could feel the
impression, like a wave of electricity, going through and
through me. Indeed, it seemed to come in waves and waves
of liquid love; for I could not express it in any other way."
—Charles Finny
describing an encounter with the Holy Spirit[10]

The Apostle Paul prayed that the believers in Ephesus would
have a revelation of how wide, deep, high and long is God's
love for them in Christ. That love is so much bigger than we
can think or imagine, yet God wants us to experience it in
greater and greater measure daily. (Ephesians 3:18) God uses
the gift He's given us called imagination.

Here's a way many of us have imagined His love:

1. If you live near a beach (the ocean or a lake) with a tem-
    perate or tropical climate, find a place at the beach where
    you can be alone.

2. Sit in the water in a position where the waves can wash
    over you safely.

3. If a lake or ocean is not available (or if it's too cold), crawl
    into a bath tub full of warm water. To help set the mood,
    use an "ocean waves" app to create the sound of waves.

4. Now imagine that the water is God's love, His unconditional, unbounded, pure, relentless, vast love for you. Imagine waves of liquid love washing over you. Delight in it as that love sweeps over your whole being, cleansing and refreshing you—love that emanates from the very heart of God. This love is greater in volume than the oceans of our planet. As you imagine God's love, know that it is God's desire to pour out His love in our hearts through His Spirit (Romans 5:5).

On a Personal Note

I am so privileged to live in Indonesia where there are beaches everywhere and the temperature is always warm enough to enjoy the ocean. Recently I was hot and tired from a long motor scooter ride on a rough road in an isolated area. I found a pristine beach with waves the perfect size for this exercise. I pulled over, stripped down to my skivvies and went for it. Heavenly!

36

TRANSFORMING YOUR MENTAL IMAGE OF GOD

The word "God" conjures up certain mental images for everyone who believes there is a God (and probably for many who say they don't believe there is a God as well). There are all kinds of those images and impressions people have about God that are not true—they don't correspond with the reality of who God is.

Coming to a relationship with Christ is the start of a journey of knowing God personally and intimately. The more we understand, follow and obey Jesus, the more we grasp the true character of God. There is a personal progressive revelation of who God really is that each of us experiences in our spiritual journey. Even after becoming a Christian and knowing things about God through the Bible, especially through what we see in Jesus from the Gospels, what we *believe* about God may be different from the mental image of God we experience on an emotional level. The following exercise will help reveal who God is to you, and hopefully, give you a clearer picture of the kind, generous, proactive, loving Father that He is.

1. Still your heart before God in a quiet place where you are completely alone. Let the peace of God completely envelope you.

2. Imagine a knock on the door. You go to open the door to find you are staring in the face of God. What is His

countenance toward you? Is He happy to see you? Is there a warmth in His eyes? A big smile? Is He reaching out to give you a bear hug? Is He eager to be invited in to spend some time with you?

3. If God's countenance toward you is anything but kind, fatherly, joyful, and full of love, then you need the Holy Spirit to give you a more accurate picture of the Father.

4. Now read the following verses aloud slowly. Then ask the Holy Spirit to give you a mental picture of God doing for you what He promises in each verse:

   - Psalm 18:19
   - Isaiah 40:11
   - Zephaniah 3:17
   - Luke 15:20-24
   - Ephesians 1:4-5
   - Ephesians 2:4-6

5. Pray in your own words something like this: "Holy Spirit, pour out the Father's love in my heart in such a way that it touches me on an emotional level. I really want to experience your fathering, kind, proactive, transforming, unconditional love for me."

6. Now wait on Him. If nothing happens immediately, pray for healing from any distorted mental image you have of God.

7. Now pray: "I pray that from your glorious, unlimited resources you will empower me with inner strength through your Spirit. I pray that Christ will make His home in my heart as I trust in you. Oh, that my roots will grow down into God's love and keep me strong. And may I have the power to understand, as all God's people should, how wide, how long, how high, and how deep your love is. May I experience the love of Christ, though it is too great

to understand fully. Then I will be made complete with all the fullness of life and power that comes from God" (paraphrase of Ephesians 3:16-19).

On a Personal Note

As a young Christ-follower doing this exercise, I would have "opened the door" to a God with a scowl on His face. I pictured God as a demanding boss who was frustrated with me because in no way was I measuring up to His standards. I was forever disappointing Him. In my case it was not because of father wounds, but rather simply bad theology in the church culture I first experienced as a Christian. It took some good teaching on the book of Romans to begin to change that distorted image. But much more significant in my transformation was the Holy Spirit encounters in which God etched into my spirit and my psyche a deep level imprint of His fatherly, kind, proactive, unconditional, transforming love for me.

37

PICTURE GOD THIS WAY

Jesus told some of His parables with the express intention of communicating to His audience what God is really like in order to combat their religious, distorted views. For example, in Luke 15 He taught that God is like a shepherd who goes after the stray sheep. He's also like a woman who loses a coin and a father who has a rebellious son. These word pictures for God were to show the most religious people of Jesus' day that God loves and even pursues sinners to seek and save them.

Very few (if any of us) have the ability to paint word pictures as effectively as Jesus. Nor do we know the Father as clearly as Jesus knew Him. However, we do have at our disposal via the internet hundreds of thousands of images of kings, fathers, judges, lions, shepherds, friends, bridegrooms, servants, women looking for something lost, and the dozens of others descriptions of God or Jesus that we find in scripture.

This next exercise is a way to create a montage of images that help us envision what God or Jesus is like.

1. Use a concordance or a Bible program online and find specific references to God/Jesus as king, father, judge, lion, shepherd, friend, bridegroom, servant, or any of the other description of Him from the Word.

2. Now look for images online of a king, a father, et cetera. A Google search will give dozens—even hundreds—to pick from. Which ones most depict who God/Jesus is to you?

3. Create an album or a presentation with the title: "How I Picture God/Jesus." Give a Bible reference for each of your entries.

4. As you review your collection, take a few minutes and acknowledge each aspect of the Lord pictured in each image. Thank Him and worship Him.

5. Now ask Him to reveal to you in a greater way how He is _____ in your life. "Lord, please show me how you are the perfect _____."

A simple variation of the above exercise would be to compile a series of video clips that depict the character of God. For example there is a YouTube video called "Team Hoyt – Redeemer." In that clip Dick Hoyt is like what I think of God pulling me or pushing me (Ricky) along in an Iron Man competition (or in my case, the race He has laid out for me. Hebrews 12:1) Several other possible clips would be those of Aragorn or Gandalf from *The Lord of the Rings*. You get the idea.

Can you see how powerful and fun it would be to share this project as a family or in your Christian community? One fun way to share it would be to flash the picture on a screen and have others guess the biblical name this image represents.

Use your favorite images on your screen saver!

On a Personal Note

Just searching for the right image, the one that best captures who God is like, was a spiritual experience for me. I avoid the religious looking ones. For example: the image I have of shepherd was not the typical blue-eyed, effeminate, well-groomed, middle-class westerner in a freshly laundered robe holding a sweet little lamb. I like the rough, tanned, muscular, disheveled, dirty-robed guy who is obviously from the Middle East.

38

A BREATH OF LIFE

And He breathed on them and said:
"Receive the Holy Spirit" (John 20:22).

This exercise is as simple as breathing. Imagine yourself inhaling life and exhaling death. With every breath, breathe in God's grace, His mercy, His forgiveness, His peace, His love, joy, and acceptance. Take a deep breath of each of these, one at a time. As you exhale, breathe out confusion, anger, resentment, disappointment, fear, worry, and restlessness.

The Hebrew term for "spirit" is *ruach*. It's the term used for the Spirit of God. It can also mean wind or breath. God desires to breath His Spirit into us each moment of our day.

On a Personal Note

If I have trouble sleeping this exercises quickly turns my anxious thoughts into peaceful sleep.

39

REVELATIONS OF GOD'S LOVE

*... and to know the King's love, though actually it's so
deep that nobody can really know it!
So may God fill you with all His fullness*
(Ephesians 3:19 TKNT).

The Apostle Paul prayed for Christ's followers in Ephesus to grasp the height, depth, width, and breadth of God's love for them (Ephesians 3: 17-19). Note, these were people who were already Christians. They had experienced God's love, but Paul was asking for a more full revelation of that love. The words to *know* and to *grasp* God's love are not referring to a mere intellectual knowledge of God. They are experiential. To be rooted and *grounded* in God's love is to **experience** His love on an emotional level in our inner being. Don't we all want this for ourselves? For those we love?

The goal of this exercise is to position ourselves for a fresh *knowing* of God's fatherly, kind, proactive, unconditional, transforming love through looking back.

1. Think back on past experiences in your life when you experienced God's love. Maybe it was a Holy Spirit encounter in a prayer time or a worship service. Perhaps you've experienced a dramatic answer to prayer that could only have been a "God thing." It could be through:

- A supernatural healing
- A moment in which your life was spared
- An amazing gift that you received
- A vision that you know was from God

There are hundreds of ways God can show us His love. The point is to think of a time when have you been deeply aware that God loves you. Pick at least five incidents from your past.

2. Try to recall what you felt before, during, and after that encounter. Were you in the middle of a tough time? Were you experiencing a great loss? Were you far from God? (I've found that most people find the answer to at least one of these three to be 'yes,' and then God breaks in with a revelation of His love.)

3. Praise Him for these revelations of His love.

4. Now ask Him for a fresh encounter with that love. Here's what I have often prayed: "Father, I open my heart for a fresh revelation of Your love for me today. May I be rooted and established in that love. May I know how high, and wide, and long, and deep is Your love for me. Let me know it not only in my head, but in my heart—to experience it—to feel it. I open my heart to receive all the love Your Holy Spirit can pour into me—Your fatherly, proactive, kind, unconditional, corrective, and transforming love. I receive today's portion of Your unfailing love. Would you surprise me with new expressions of your love? "Show me Your unfailing love in wonderful ways" (Psalm 17:7). Pray this kind of prayer in your own words, in your own way.

On a Personal Note

My most dramatic encounters with God's love have come when I was least expecting them. One happened the night I learned of my dad's sudden death of a heart attack. He was thirty-nine years old and I was only seventeen. Dad had just divorced my step-mother and we were to move into an apartment together the day after my graduation from high school six weeks later. My mother had died when I was three, and my dad's two subsequent marriages had failed.

On that faithful day, after the initial shock and tears, people started showing up expressing their condolences. My dad was well-known in our community. After everyone had left, I drove out into the country and stood out in an open field and cried out to God in my grief. God showed up. He spoke to me (not audibly) of His love for me. He told me He would be a father to me. He would provide for me and counsel me. He would be more to me than any earthly father could be. I wept, overwhelmed by a sense of His presence and comfort. That encounter shaped my life, my destiny.

EXERCISES THAT OVERCOME ANXIETY AND STRESS

40

PALMS UP, PALMS DOWN, PALMS UP

Give all of your worries and cares to God,
for He cares for you
(1 Peter 5:7).

Inspired by Richard Foster's classic book *The Celebration of Discipline* over 30 years ago, I began practicing and teaching Palms Up, Palms Down. Inadvertently, I have added another step. I didn't realize until I wrote this book that I had altered his original version that supposedly dates back hundreds of years. O well, I like mine better!

Here's how it goes:

1. Find a comfortable sitting position in a room that's quiet and where you can be alone. Still your soul and imagine Jesus standing right in front of you.

2. Place your hands on your knees, palms facing up. Envision your hands holding the things that are heavy for you now. What's keeping you awake at night? What is it that's making your jaw tense? What's weighing on your thoughts and affecting you emotionally, even robbing you of joy or peace? Put every negative, troubling thing you can think of in those hands.

3. Now slowly turn your palms down letting everything you've "put in your hands" to fall to the floor, at the feet of Jesus. Imagine Him saying "I've got this," and picking up all the things you were carrying. Let yourself experience the lightness of soul of having transferred all that baggage you were carrying into His care.

4. Once you've enjoyed this tangible lightness of soul for a few minutes, smile at Him and tell Him how much you love and appreciate Him taking care of all these things.

5. Now, turn your palms back up to receive what He wants to place in them. Imagine receiving His righteousness, His peace, His promises, and His unconditional love. He may have something else for you. Receive it and relish it.

6. Again smile at Him and thank Him.

How often should you do this exercise? As often you find yourself carrying things that He is much better at handling. How often should you do this exercise? Whenever you are ready to exchange a weary and burdened heart for a rested one (Matthew 11:28-30).

On a Personal Note

When I've been anxious or burdened this exercise provides an immediate sense of lightness of soul, a tangible relief. I have occasionally experienced a relapse–after a couple of hours I find myself feeling the weight of my situation or challenge. I simply pause and reenact this process of transferring my cares to Him.

41

TELLING GOD
HOW YOU FEEL

I will be glad and rejoice in your unfailing love,
for you have seen my troubles,
and you care about the anguish of my soul
(Psalm 31:7 NLT).

We know God cares about what we are facing, what we are struggling with, and what we feel. David knew how to express his emotions to God, even emotions of despair and anguish. In modern terms we could say David knew how "to connect with God on an emotional level." Here's a way we can do the same:

1. Still your heart before God.

2. Ask yourself: What are the emotions that have been stirring around in my heart? What do I feel right now?

3. Write it down as a letter or email to God. "God, I feel _____." It can be anything: fear, disappointment, regret, excitement, shame, discouragement, anger, resentment, joy, or even hopelessness. Be honest. Don't be surprised if you have several emotions going on at once. There may even be conflicting emotions.

4. If you have an idea of why you feel that way, express it to God. If not, it is no big deal. Avoid psychoanalyzing

yourself. It's much more helpful to lay out these emotions to God, however raw they are. He can handle it.

5. Now ask: "Father, what would you say to the _____ I'm experiencing right now?" Wait on Him and write out any impression that seems to correspond to God's character which we see in the Word.

6. Verbalize what you have written.

Even though God knows the depth of our every emotion (and the reason behind them), it is so important to be transparent and honest with Him in expressing them, however negative these emotions may be. You will find this simple exercise far more helpful (and cheaper) than the best therapist around!

On a Personal Note

I followed Christ for decades before I could totally be free to open up to God about my negative emotions. I was so afraid God would be angry or disappointed with me. Of course, just the opposite occurred. I felt His presence, His counsel, and His comfort in every emotional state I've experienced. Such freedom!

42

Cast Your Cares
on HIM

Cast all your anxiety on Him because He cares for you
(1 Peter 5:7).

Much (if not all) our anxiety is caused by carrying things we were not meant to carry. We all know we ought to cast our cares upon the Lord. He has told that worry is unnecessary, unhelpful, and unnatural for a Christ-follower (Matthew 6:25-34), but it's challenging to truly relinquish every care into the hands of the Lord.

Here's a prayer exercise that will help:

1. Think through what's troubling you. What's causing you anxiety or stress? What's keeping you awake at night?

2. Create an "altar" in your house: a bed, a couch, a table. Imagine this "altar" is a holy place like the one in the Old Testament times where sacrifices are brought before the Lord. It's a place where a transaction takes place. It's a place where what is yours becomes God's.

3. Now find any object you can carry (a pillow, a book, a picture, a purse, etc.) Imagine this object to be one of the burdens or cares that has been weighing on you.

4. Bring it to your "altar" and offer it to God in a priestly fashion. Give words to what you are doing, such as: "Father,

this pillow represents my son and the relationship with the girl he is dating. I now bring this concern to you. I offer it to you. Please take it from me. Please exercise your kingly authority in this relationship. It's yours and not mine."

5. If you have other worries, offer them to God in like manner.

6. You will probably experience significant relief. Thank God for taking your burdens.

7. It is likely that you will want to "pick up" the burden again at some point in your day. If so, repeat the process.

On a Personal Note

I first prayed this way when I was dating Janine (my wife of 40+ years now). As our relationship developed, I began to feel strongly that she was the girl for me. I found myself trying to figure it out more than I should, so I decided to bring these thoughts to the Lord every time I began to think them. If I happened to be at home I would go into my bedroom, take up my pillow and offer her and our relationship andour future together (or apart) to God. "Here she is, Lord. She's way more beautiful than this pillow. I entrust our plans fully to You." The relief was immediate and tangible.

43

A CHRISTIAN
MANTRA

Set your minds on things above, not on earthly things.
For you died, and your life is now hidden with Christ in God
(Colossians 3:2-3).

We typically associate the term *mantra* with eastern religions. I have dozens of Hindu friends who practice mantras in an effort to invite the presence of their gods or goddesses. Often these mantras are repetitive phrases (often melodic) that express a human longing for truth, reality, light, peace, love, and knowledge.

As Christians we can relate to these longings. For centuries Jesus followers have expressed such longings to the God of heaven through these phrases. The key difference is that we do not repeat these words or phrases as a magic formula in order to conjure up a hypnotic state, but rather to set our minds on God and pour out our hearts to Him.

This is simply a technique to center our hearts on the living God and experience His peace.

1. Find a comfortable sitting position in a room that is quiet where you are alone.

2. Settle your thoughts for a few moments, allowing your breathing to slow down and your body to relax.

3. Chose a phrase that expresses a truth about God: *God you are faithful. God, you are my perfect father. You are love*, for example. Ideally you would choose a reality statement that counters some lie you have been believing about God. If you have been thinking that your performance isn't measuring up or that you are not worthy enough to be loved by God, you might choose a phrase like: *You love me just as I am.*

4. Repeat your phrase slowly, bringing the mantra in sync with your breathing. For example, you could say "You love me" as you inhale and "just as I am" as you exhale.

5. Continue this practice for a few minutes. Over time your heart and mind will began to shift toward this reality. You will know this exercise is being used by the Holy Spirit if you begin to experience His peace and love more than when you began.

6. After ten to fifteen minutes of repeating a phrase about God, pick a longing of your heart, like: *Come and fill me with your love. I open my heart to all love you want to pour into it.* If you find yourself longing for joy, peace, faith, or boldness, ask for it a simple prayer of repetition.

7. Repeat this longing of your heart until your heart is fully confident that God is filling you with the thing you lack in yourself.

On a Personal Note

I have been one of those Christians who have shied away from anything associated with eastern religions, mantras included. However, I came across Mark Thibodeaux's clear explanation of a Christian version of a mantra in his book *Armchair Mystic*.[11] I gave the above exercise a try and loved it. I since have been astounded by the number of devotional masters of previous centuries who practiced this regularly.

44

A BIBLICAL SABBATH

Remember the Sabbath day by keeping it holy.
Six days you shall labor and do all your work, but
the seventh day is a Sabbath to the Lord our God
(Exodus 20:8-10).

For many of us, doing nothing productive for a 24-hour period every week is as antiquated, weird, and unnecessary as using a horse and buggy as our main mode of transportation. Christians who are rigid about "keeping" the Sabbath tend to fall into legalism. So why go there? However, when you discover the power of a weekly day of rest and restoration, you will realize why God instituted this pattern for our well-being.

We could discuss the *why* behind a Sabbath at length, but better yet, let's DO a Sabbath similar to the original intent God had for His people when Moses was given the ten commandments.

1. Select a suitable 24-hour period that starts around 6 to7 p.m. Depending on the typical demands in your week, Friday or Saturday evening may be the best start time (neither of those days worked for me as a pastor so I chose Thursday evening until Friday evening).

2. Jewish people have a traditional meal as a family to launch into their Sabbath. Their special meal involved lighting candles, reading the Scripture, giving thanks, and speaking a blessing over the children. Try this.

3. During the 24-hours you have set aside as a Sabbath, give yourself permission to rest from work, physical exhaustion, hurriedness, worry, decision-making, and running errands.

4. Avoid work-related emails and phone calls. If possible, don't even think about work.

5. Linger in your devotional time. Choose a couple of the exercises you've found helpful in this book. We're not talking about religious striving, but rather nurturing a sense of God's presence.

6. Take time to delight in God's creation and its gifts. Take in the beauty of nature. Stop and smell the flowers, literally.

7. Give yourself permission to pursue hobbies that are restorative.

8. Delight in people. Slow down and connect with the people you normally don't have time to talk to.

9. Sleep late and then take a nap (if you can).

10. Play. Have fun. Whatever you enjoy, be it sports, dancing, going to museums, or flying a kite, imbibe in it with pleasure.

I like what Peter Scazzaro says: "Sabbath is like receiving the gift of a heavy snow day every week. Stores are closed. Roads are impassable. Suddenly you have the gift of a day to do whatever you want. You don't have any obligations, pressures, or responsibilities. You have permission to play, be with friends, take a nap, read a good book. Few us would give ourselves a 'no obligation day' very often. God gives us one—every seventh day." [12]

On a Personal Note

By God's grace I learned this discipline in my early twenties. I was a full time seminary student and worked fifteen to twenty hours a week. In addition, I was married and had an infant daughter. My friends thought I was crazy for setting aside twenty-four hours every week to do nothing related to my studies or work and just enjoy being with my family (and God). I made good grades, kept my job, and my family thrived. It's a pattern I have maintained for the last forty years. Stress has been minimal. Burnout, non-existent. As far as my emotional health, I feel healthy... (though you may need to ask my wife about that). I am confident that this is due, in part, to a lifestyle of Sabbath.

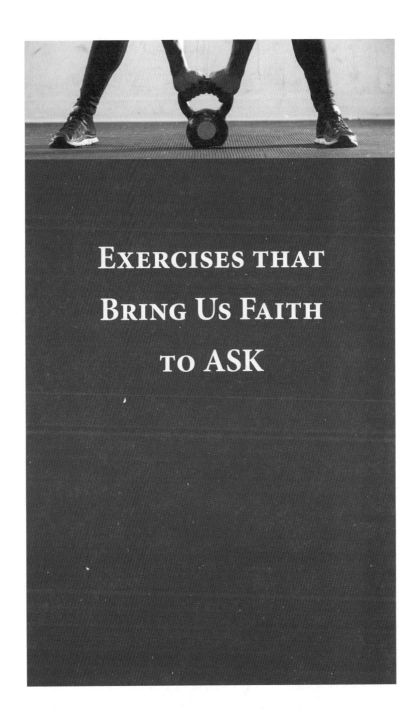

EXERCISES THAT BRING US FAITH TO ASK

45

TOP TEN ANSWERED PRAYERS

He replied, "Because you have so little faith.
Truly I tell you, if you have faith as small as a mustard seed,
you can say to this mountain, 'Move from here to there,'
and it will move. Nothing will be impossible for you"
(Matthew 17:20).

I was sharing with a Muslim friend and referenced the ways God has so graciously answered so many of my prayers. He asked: "For example?" I stumbled momentarily and came up with a several answers. Then I thought: I have journals full of answered prayers. I must not forget these powerful ways God has demonstrated His love and mercy in my life. Later, I was wondering what have been my top ten most significant answers to prayer. What are some of the breakthroughs I've known that couldn't be explained any other way other than God did it!? There are miraculous ways God has answered some of the bold, specific requests in times of desperation in fulfillment of my B.H.A.P. - Big Harry Audacious Prayers.[13]

1. Find a time and place where you can be alone for at least an hour. Center your heart through prayers of gratitude, adoration, and submission.

2. Now make a list of you top ten answers to prayer. If you can't think of ten just list all that come to mind. Recount how you felt upon hearing about each breakthrough.

3. Is there a pattern, a common "grace" you have to believe God for certain needs? For example, I have multiple ex-

amples of financial breakthroughs and couples who have been able to have children after prayer, even though they had previously had trouble conceiving.

4. In light of these powerful demonstrations of God's power and mercy in your past, what happens to your faith for the "not-yet-breakthroughs" you are facing right now?

5. What about ways that God has blessed you that you didn't even ask for? List those out in your prayer journal.

6. Recount those blessings through prayers of gratitude.

Note: I included question number five because many of God's most gracious gifts in my life have come my way without me even asking and certainly without me deserving them.

On a Personal Note

One of my top ten: when we were pastors in Austin, Texas, Janine was driving a car with over 200,000 miles on it because we had given away her car fund for our church's building program. The car fund was slowly being replenished but I kept asking God for a newer low-mileage car that would be a sign of His favor because of her sacrificial generosity. One day, our friend Debbie was proudly showing Janine her new Nissan Murano. Janine celebrated with her and while driving home felt sincere gratitude for her old car that was still plugging along with very few maintenance issues. As Debbie was driving home God spoke to her to give Janine her car. Three days later Debbie handed Janine the keys and the title to a car worth more than $32,000 with only 400 miles on it! She even made sure we didn't have to pay for the taxes on it. Tears come to mind as I recount it.

This exercise is extremely faith-building for obvious reasons. It's powerful to remember these stories and even more rewarding to share them with others.

46

Praying with Gall

I tell you, even though he will not get up
and give you the bread because of friendship,
yet because of your shameless audacity he will surely
get up and give you as much as you need
(Luke 11:8).

Although Jesus prayed a lot, He didn't actually say that much about prayer. Out of dozens of parables He told, only two were about how to pray, one in Luke 11 and the other in Luke 18. This exercise and the following are applications of what He taught in these parables.

The parable in Luke 11:5-8 is about a man who needs to feed his guest so he goes to a neighbor and ask for three loaves of bread. He gets what he asks for because of his boldness. The word *boldness* in this passage is from a Greek word, *anaidian*, that's a challenge to translate because the word is used nowhere else in the New Testament. However, the opposite form of the word is used when Paul describes how godly women should act—with propriety, politely.[14] The *ana* prefix in the Luke 11:8 word makes it negative. It literally means impropriety or rudeness. We would use the word *gall*.

So Jesus is saying that this is how we are to pray—*with gall!* Like the man in the story, we are invited to (or more like encouraged to) ask very specifically for things that we don't deserve irrespective of the "will" of the one from whom we ask.

With that kind of gall ...

1. Make a list of your heart's desires. Don't be timid. Don't be vague. Be specific and bold to write out what you ask God for as if you had the freedom to approach Him with such requests—because you do!

2. Your petitions might be related to relational goals, health, challenges with work, education or career. If you have financial needs, be specific. Are you single and wish to be married? Ask not only for a spouse, but ask for the kind of spouse you seek. Ask for things that seem impossible. Ask for things you've never really asked for, but have definitely wanted.

3. It's not necessary to feel a lot of faith for these requests. Your faith is in the asking.

4. After you listed at least ten items, read your list out loud to God. Thank Him for the privilege of asking. Thank Him that He hears these requests. Tell Him you are bringing these things before Him as a child would ask for an ice cream or a pizza from his dad. Be honest if you don't feel a lot of faith. Ask Him for faith.

5. Keep your list assessable. You will want to come back to these requests. I have mine in my prayer journal and a soft copy on my computer. I put a ☐ in front of my request so I go back and can check the box when it is answered.

On a Personal Note

This freedom to petition God with bold, specific requests is something Janine and I learned to do early in our marriage. It all began when we were driving across the desert of Arizona pulling a U-Haul trailer which contained all of our worldly possessions (the smallest of trailers in the lot). We were moving from Austin, Texas to Pasadena, California where I was to attend Fuller Seminary. We were in our early twenties with a nine-month old infant. We wrote out five specific requests we had for this huge and challenging transition. Things like jobs, childcare, a church community, and more. were on our list. Only, there were a lot of qualifiers like: "We ask for a two-bedroom apartment close to campus for $200/month or less!" I can't say we were overflowing with confidence as we wrote out these petitions. However, four of the five were answered to the "T" within a week! The fifth one was answered within a month!

47

PERSISTENT PRAYER

Then Jesus told His disciples a parable to show that they should always pray and not give up
(Luke 18:1).

The big-idea Jesus was communicating in the parable of the persistent widow (Luke 18:1-9) was no mystery—*keep* asking. Be persistent. God is not like the unjust judge, but our petitions often need to be expressed again and again. Too often we give up. Jesus asks an interesting question at the end of this parable: *When the Son of Man comes, will He find faith on the earth?* "Faith" here means "asking again." There's faith when we ask and there's also faith, possibly even more faith, in *asking again.*

Here is a way to practice this kind of faith.

1. Take your list from the previous exercise and repeat the process of presenting your petitions to God.

2. Ask the Holy Spirit to bring to mind requests from the past that you've given up on. Be bold to "resubmit" these desires of your heart.

3. Try taking the example of the widow literally: *And will not God bring about justice for His chosen ones, who cry out to Him day and night?* Pray your list day and night until you experience breakthrough. Some have used the acronym P.U.S.H.—Pray Until Something Happens.

4. It's important that you vocalize these longings of your heart, not just think them. The widow did cry out to Jesus.

On a Personal Note

I've never been able to figure out why some of my petitions are answered immediately and why some that I've prayed for years remain unanswered. From this story I find a lot of freedom to keep asking. My prayer journal can attest to some prayers that I've prayed for years that suddenly, with seemingly very little confidence or faith on my part, just happened.

48

IMAGES OF THE
LONGINGS OF YOUR HEART

There are images that sometimes capture the longings of our hearts more than words can express. Even if you are more verbal than visual, a picture may be worth a thousand words. For example, one day I noticed a papaya tree that was laden with more papayas than you would normally see on three trees. There were at least twenty-five huge papayas hanging there in near perfect symmetry and several were so ripe that they could fall at any moment. I immediately said, "Lord, that's how I want my life to be: full of ripe juicy fruit! And lots of it." I captured the moment on my cell phone camera. Pulling it up and viewing it again it reignites that familiar plea.

This exercise is a way in which you can convey some of the deepest longings of your heart to the Father.

1. Read Mark 10:46-52. When you read Jesus' question to Bartimaeus, imagine Him asking you that same question. Instead of answering with words, come up with a photo or video clip that would say it better than words.

2. Use the internet to look for the visual image that best expresses your longings. If you have a talent for drawing, create the image yourself.

3. Put together a collage, an album, or a PowerPoint presentation.

4. Now scroll from photo to photo or video clip to video clip and give a *presentation for God* expressing what you want most on life.

5. You can share your presentation with your family or your Christian community as a way to invite them into your longings.

On a Personal Note

Here are several more images from my album that might help your creative juices flow: a painting of a group of workers harvesting rice, a group of young men and women wearing Muslim clothing dancing with abandonment before the throne of God in heaven, and a photo of a man standing with a bull horn in a crowded Asian market.

49

A 21-Day PUSH

Keep on asking, and you will receive what you ask for.
Keep on seeking, and you will find. Keep on knocking,
and the door will be open to you
(Luke 11:9).

One simple way to "keep on" with our request is to identify a handful of longings or needs and then commit to pray often for these requests for a 21-day period. There is nothing magic about twenty-one days, but a story in the Book of Daniel in which he prays intently for that amount of time has inspired many of us.[15] Often something happens within twenty-one days of this kind of fervent petition. Here is one way we tried this:

1. Take time to come up with a list of three to seven longings or needs that you, or someone you know, has. We call them "not-yet-breakthroughs." It could be anything that has come to mind in the previous two exercises.

2. Write the prayer on a colored sticker or dot (round sticker) small enough to stick on your cell phone. Just write one or two words representing that need like: Dave, loan, car, job, David's passport, or whatever represents the request.

3. For the next three weeks, pray for those needs every time you use your cell phone.

4. Peel the dots or stickers off as prayers are answered.

On a Personal Note

My breakthrough prayers included a friend who was critically ill, a car for a team member who had nothing to pay toward the purchase, a passport that was desperately needed but "lost" in the administrative shuffle, a job for our son, and breakthrough for a family facing major roadblocks in an international adoption. All but one dot was removed during the 21-day period!

Imagine: What if a church or a small group community did this exercise together? What a spirit of celebration would be ours if we all had just one breakthrough!

50

Expressing Your
Disappointments

*I pour out my complaints before Him
and tell Him all my troubles*
(Psalm 142:2).

What if you ask boldly and persistently and nothing happens? You ask again. But what if the desire you've offered to God doesn't happen and seemingly will never happen? For example, you are in a financial crisis and you petition God for a financial miracle and yet you lose your house. Or you pray for someone who is ill and that person dies. These are the times one must learn to lament. The Psalms are full of prayers of **lament**. Some are communal expressions of grief or sorrow. Others are individuals like David asking God why misfortune has come his way or *why* his prayers haven't been answered. Nearly every lament in the Bible turns into an expression of worship or trust.

Here's an exercise in lament:

1. If lamenting seems unspiritual or disrespectful of God, read some of the examples in Psalms (Psalm 22, 72, 3, 5, 39, 54).

2. In your own words, express your disappointment, sorrow or grief to God. "Father, I'm really disappointed that _____. I felt like I was fol-

lowing/obeying you and yet look what's happened. Why?
I ask you for _____ and was so
hopeful that you would come through."

3. If you write it in your prayer journal, be sure to express it
orally as well.

4. Now wait in His presence. It's not uncommon for trust and
praise to well up, even out of those places of disappointment.

5. Even if you don't feel victorious or joyful after you have
expressed your grief, sorrow, or disappointment to God,
you will at least have greater intimacy and integrity in
your relationship with Him. You can choose to trust Him
in your disappointments.

On a Personal Note

The freedom to lament creates a greater freedom to ask
boldly. It frees us from the fear that in not getting what we ask
our relationship with God will be damaged or undermined. It
is just the opposite. Often dramatic breakthroughs have come
after I have communicated my disappointments to God. Sometimes there is still no answer to my petition, but I've grown to
trust Him more. There is always a sense of experiencing His
comfort, His presence, and greater faith when I've lamented
in the way described above.

51

PRAYING THE PROMISES

My heart is confident in you,
O God, my heart is confident.
No wonder I can sing your praises
(Psalm 57:7 NLT).

Nothing is more encouraging than when someone you love communicates their trust in you. "I know you will do the right thing." "I had no doubt that you would follow through on that commitment." "I knew you would be there for me." So true, right? God seems to delight in our trust in Him and His promises as well. Declaring your confidence in God's promises is not only an expression of faith but also a form of worship and gratitude.

Here's a powerful way to convey to God our confidence and trust in Him:

1. Start a list of your favorite promises that God has made in His Word. When you come across another one, add it to your list. If none come to mind, here are a few you can start with:

   - You will fulfill your purpose for me (Psalm 57:2).

   - You will supply all my needs according to your riches in glory (Philippians 4:19).

   - You are with me to the ends of the earth (Psalm 139:8-9).

- As I abide in you and your word abides in me I will bear fruit (John 15:5).

2. Now speak out that promise as a prayer of praise. "I will praise God for what He has promised" (Psalm 56:4). Personalize these promises.

3. Keep a running list. Add to it as you come across a new promise in your Bible reading.

4. Pray them often.

On a Personal Note

I started my list more than fifteen years ago. I currently have compiled more than seventy-five promises! The list continues to grow (see Appendix B for an example of ten of these promises). I pray this list at least once a week. It builds my faith like no other exercise.

One example: Last week I was struck by this familiar statement in the oft-quoted twenty-third Psalm; *You lead me in paths of righteousness for Your name's sake.* (Psalm 23:3 NIV) I had such peace and confidence as I declared it specifically in application to some of the decisions I am facing.

52

BEING HONEST ABOUT YOUR DOUBTS

Immediately the boy's father exclaimed, "I do believe;
help me overcome my unbelief!"
(Mark 9:24).

I have serious doubts about a Christian who says they never have doubts. All of us experience some level of doubt. At the very least, we have to acknowledge there is some level of "unbelief" in our own faith in asking God for some things, sometimes. God is not angry or even unsettled when we acknowledge our doubts. In fact, He delights in honest hearts. And He can meet us in our sincere struggles at believing Him.

The following exercise is a way we can identify and acknowledge some of our doubts and then look to Him to change us.

1. Still your heart before God. Have some writing material to use for taking notes. Your prayer journal would work well here.

2. Spend some time in prayers of gratitude and adoration.

3. Now, ask the Holy Spirit to show or remind you of doubts that have recently surfaced in your thoughts. No need to go there with doubts from the past; just stick with the current ones.

4. You can be totally honest. "Father, I struggle with believing…." "I find myself seriously doubting…" List all that come to mind.

5. Now ask: "What would you say to my doubts?" Wait and write what God seems to be saying. If you hear nothing, don't worry. If you doubt that what comes to mind is really from God, write it down anyway.

6. Even if God doesn't seem to be saying something to your doubts in the moment, He has probably has said something in His Word that counters that doubt. Look up a promise in that Bible that speaks to your doubt. For example, you may say: "I have serious doubts that I will ever get out of debt. I've prayed about this so many times and nothing has changed." Now find one of the promises in the Bible that says the opposite, like: *"My God shall supply all of your needs according to His riches in glory."* (Philippians 4:19)

7. Now, out loud, as a sincere prayer, tell God your doubt but then add to it: "I really want to believe that You will supply my needs so I can pay off this debt. Help my unbelief. With all the faith I can muster I say: You shall supply all of my needs according to your riches in glory! I choose to believe this even though it doesn't feel like I really believe it."

8. Monitor your heart. What happened when you laid this out before God? David said: "When doubts filled my mind, your comfort gave me renewed hope and cheer" (Psalm 94:19 NLT).

9. Work through your list of doubts as time permits.

Imagine how powerful this exercise with be in a community of loving, faith-filled Christ-followers. Often others have faith for the very areas in which I struggle.

On a Personal Note

The week before penning this exercise I had a chest cold. I never get over chest colds without antibiotics. Day after day I felt it getting worse, but I held out taking meds because I wanted to do my weekly fast. I "felt" very little faith when I asked the Lord to heal me without taking antibiotics. My prayer was short and went something like this: "Father, you know how little faith I have as I ask this, but would you just clear this up without me taking pills?" I really don't know how much faith I lacked or had in that prayer. God is the perfect faith-judge. I'm not. But He had mercy and I recovered without medication.

53

THE THINGS I WANT MOST IN LIFE

Each of us have longings that no one else knows about. I'm talking about dreams that remain hidden, not because they are sinister or unholy, but because they are secret desires. You dare not talk about them because they seem too grandiose, even outrageous, to verbalize. Think of it like your spiritual bucket list.

In this exercise you will identify some of them and express them to God.

1. With a pen in hand (or on your laptop) start this sentence: "What I really want most in life is…" Now finish the sentence. It may be helpful to think along the lines of relationships, career, lifestyle, accomplishments, legacy, or even your relationship with God. Let your heart dream.

2. Take the time you need to come up with at least five, but no more than ten, things that you really want in life.

3. Once you've written them down, verbalize them as a list of prayers. Expound on them, one by one.

4. Now ask the Father: "What do you think about these longings?" "Are these the thing You want for me?" "What am I missing?"

5. Write down what you hear.

6. Create a document that you can easily access and re-pray when these longings come to mind.

On a Personal Note

I found it really easy to come up with ten things I really want before I die. I'm going out on a limb to give you a couple examples from my list but hopefully your list will seem a bit less bizarre after hearing a couple of mine. "Lord, I want to pray for a blind person and have them see." And this one: "Lord, please give me the opportunity to give away over a million dollars to empower the poor to create income streams that enrich their lives."

EXERCISES THAT BRING US JOY

54

JOYFUL MEMORIES

*Our mouths were filled with laughter, our tongues
with songs of joy. Then it was said among the nations,
"The LORD has done great things for them"*
(Psalms 126:2).

This Psalm was written to celebrate an event in history when the Israelites returned home from exile. The author was saying: "Wasn't that amazing?" "Wasn't God so good to us?" He was caught up in a joyful memory and knew that it was because of Yahweh's great love they had experienced the gift of being able to return to Zion. The ancient Jewish culture was much better at retelling and reliving the moments in their history when God blessed them than we are. They knew how to celebrate.

We can learn through simple exercises like the following:

With a pen and your prayer journal (or on your laptop), list every joyful memory that comes to mind. Don't limit your memories to "spiritual" events in your life. Go back as far as you can remember. You should be able to come up with at least a dozen in the first 30 minutes. You may need several rounds of this. Try for thirty minutes or so a day for several days.

On a Personal Note

More than thirty joyful memories came to mind in less than thirty minutes. Some of the memories were repeated experiences like watching the sun come up from a tree stand while hunting in the woods of East Texas in Autumn. There are dozens of pleasant memories tied to that piece of land that has been in my family for 140 years. I couldn't wipe a smile off my face while giving myself to remembering these joyful events in my life. I filled up more than three pages with these memories in the initial go-round. Others surfaced in the weeks that followed.

55

Drilling Down into a Joyful Memory

... so that they may have the full measure
of my joy within them
(John 17:13).

Jesus delights in bringing us His joy. Not just a smattering, but the full measure of His joy. The following exercise will help us experience that joy. The past gifts of joy can be relived and savored so as to impact our present joy.

Here's how it goes.

1. Take one of your favorite joyful memories.

2. Relive that memory by placing yourself back into the event. Remember every detail that comes to mind. Focus on the unmitigated joy of the experience. Let your mind go there for at least ten minutes. Let yourself smile or even laugh at the memory.

3. Now ask Jesus: "Where were You as I was having so much fun?" "In what way were You sharing Your joy with me in that experience?" Expect Him to answer you.

4. Then ask, "How would you want to share your joy with me in my current circumstance?" Be attentive to His answer.

5. Write it in red in your prayer journal. Then share it with your family and/or Christian community.

On a Personal Note

One day my friend Craig gave me his car. It wasn't just any 'ol car. It was a Honda Del Sol. He was getting a new one and knew that I enjoyed driving his sports car with the top down. So, he graciously handed me the key one day after a game of racquetball l and said "It's yours." I was elated. With the top down I sang praises all the way home. I'm sure people thought I was nuts. That car was such a blast to drive, especially in the spring in central Texas when the wild flowers were in bloom. When I asked the Lord: "Where were You as I was having so much fun?" He said: "Riding there in the front seat beside you enjoying the flowers."

56

A Prayer for More Joy

Do you ever find joy to be illusive? I do. In 1998 I came to the sobering realization that I was not nearly as joyful as I had been in my past, even though I had so many things going for me. I found myself asking the Lord about it and pleading with Him to restore my joy. Using a concordance software program, I looked up every reference in Scripture with the words joy or rejoice. I printed them out and read them out loud as personalized prayers. I then created a crafted prayer (see Exercise 96) and began to pray it often.

Here's a way you can begin to ask for more joy:

1. Look up the following passages: Hebrews 1:9; John 15:11; 16:24; 17:13; Luke 1:14; Matthew 13:44; Romans 14:17; 1 Peter 1:8; Psalm 16:11; 30:11; 126:3

2. Read them slowly and turn them into prayers of praise and gratitude. Take note of:

   • God's or Jesus' joy.
   • Their delight in sharing that joy with us.
   • The promises of joy.

3. Express to God any way in which you may not be experiencing that joy.

4. Now ask Him for that joy: Here are a couple of verses that help in the asking: Psalm 35:27; 51:12; 86:4; 90:14

5. Ask Him what changes you need to make in your life that that will help you experience more of His joy. I'm finding that
    - when I invest in the lives of others I find greater joy;
    - when I overflow with gratitude toward Him and others I find greater joy;
    - when I lavish Him with praise I find greater joy;
    - when I surrender everything to Him, when I lose my life, I find it and also find greater joy.

6. It may be deep-level healing or deliverance that you need to be free to embrace His joy. Ask Him to lead you to the right resources, counselor, doctors, et cetera so that these prayers won't be hindered by any internal baggage or even chemical or nutritional imbalances in your body.

7. Finally, choose joy. You can exercise the joy muscle by choosing to be happy in Him.

On a Personal Note

As I began to pray for more joy there were no immediate, dynamic breakthroughs. But I did notice a heightened sense of what actually brings me greater joy. There were no "three simple steps to greater joy," but I found as I turned my heart to God throughout each day through the exercises I have compiled in this book, I became more joy-filled. I became more aware of how my joy increased in direct proportion to my obedience to God. I've included my current crafted prayer for joy in Appendix C. I say "current" because it has been updated and revised a dozen times since the first draft was written eighteen years ago.

57

ACTIVATE HOPE

*The widow who is really in need and left all alone
puts her hope in God and continues night and
day to pray and to ask God for help*
(1 Timothy 5:5).

Everyone believes hope is a good thing. Many speak of hope as something that you may or may not have, as if it were in your genetic make-up (or not). But we can choose to hope. As Christians we believe hope has an object: God. Like the widow mentioned in 1 Timothy, we too place our hope *in God*. There's a radical difference between *hoping things will get better* and *putting our hope in God to make them better*. We can purposely, actively, tangibly put our hope in God.

Here's a practical way we can choose to hope in God.

1. Find a time and place where you can be alone for at least an hour. Center your heart through prayers of gratitude, adoration, and submission.

2. Consider: What are places in your life that seem rather hopeless? You may have given up believing that this will ever change. Francis Frangipane says: "If there is any area of your life that doesn't glisten with hope, then you are believing a lie and that area is a stronghold of the devil in your life."[16] It could be:

- Your financial situation
- A health issue
- Your marriage, or the prospect of getting married
- Your relationship with your parents, or your kids
- Your career
- Your weight
- The salvation of a friend or family member
- A dream or longing of your heart that you've pleaded with God to bring about but at this point it seems it will never happen

3. Once you've identified the places in your life that don't glisten with hope, be totally honest with God it. If it's easier, write it out in your prayer journal first, then say it to God.

4. Now read the following passages of Scripture and turn them into personal prayers in light of your longing for fresh hope:

- Psalm 43:5, 42:5,11; 31:24; 33:18
- Romans 8:24-25; 12:12; 15:13
- Ephesians 1:18

5. Think about the widow mentioned in 1 Timothy 5:5. How desperate was she? What did she do to put her hope in God? How might her example change how *we put our hope in God*?

6. Write out a Crafted Prayer for Hope. (Follow the steps in exercise 96.) This last step may take you several more one-hour prayer sessions.

On a Personal Note

There's always more "glisten" to my hope when I pray my crafted prayers for hope. The challenge is that in the heat of the day my sense of hopelessness surfaces again. The growing edge of my faith is to identify when the glisten is fading and pause to my hope in God... again.

58

WHAT I HAVE TO LOOK
FORWARD TO

*But we are looking forward to the new heavens and new earth
He has promised, a world filled with God's righteousness* (2
Peter 3:13).

Joy comes through anticipation. No matter how hard life
is at the moment, filling our hearts and thoughts with the
expectation of what's going to happen that will be fun, fulfill-
ing and pleasurable sparks joy. It's easy to be joyful when we
have something we look forward to. Hope in the Bible is the
confident expectation of God breaking into every realm of our
existence and establishing His kingly reign.

This next exercise will help you experience the joy that the
God of hope wants to give you.

1. From what you have read in the Bible, what do have to look
   forward to? Here are a few references that will help jog your
   memory: 1 Corinthians 15:23-28, 42-44; 2 Corinthians
   3:18; 4:17; 5:4-5; Romans 8:18; 1 Thessalonians 4:15-17;
   2 Timothy 4:8; 2 Peter 3:13; Revelation 11:15; 20:6,10

2. Look up the references and make a list of what we have to
   look forward to. Add other aspects of the hope we have in
   the future that the Lord has for us.

3. Now read your list out loud as a hope-filled prayer.

4. If your "joy-level" isn't increasing, then read it again (imagine the excitement of a 6-year old at Christmas).

5. Add to this list as you come across other Bible promises of our future.

6. When you are tempted to think that such promises are "a long way off," remember: With the Lord a day is like a thousand years, and a thousand years are like a day (2 Peter 3:8).

On a Personal Note

Here are a few of the things to look forward to on my list:

- In just a very short time I will be either welcoming Your royal appearing on earth or taking my last breath and being welcomed where You are.
- Living forever on a new, pristine planet earth without pollution of any kind.
- Exchanging this old, decaying, shabby body for a new, heavenly one.

I've also made a list of "what I have to look forward to before I die (or before He returns)". For example, this is what I have recorded and re-pray from time to time:

"In faith, before that time, while I am in this present evil age:

- I will have a life FULL of righteousness, peace, and joy in the Holy Spirit.
- I will bear much fruit, bringing great glory to God.
- I will experience your sweet presence in whatever sorrows or pleasures, failure or success, struggles or victories I experience.
- I will become more and more like Jesus.
- I will be deeply satisfied in you every morning and sing for joy throughout every day."

I have at least a dozen other things on my list, but you get the picture.

59

LAUGHING AT THE LIES

One of Satan's schemes is to plant lies into our thoughts. Remember the Garden of Eden? We've all heard Satan's lies about God, about ourselves, about our circumstances, and about many things. At any given time, each of us are hearing a certain set of lies from our enemy. Defeat, hopelessness, unbelief, and confusion grow in us when we start believing those lies. Here's an exercise that will help us counter those lies and bring an incredible amount of joy in the process.

1. Take some time to pray prayers of gratitude and adoration.

2. Center your heart on God's empowering presence.

3. What are the lies you've been hearing lately? It is not important to debate whether these came from Satan or your fleshly way of thinking.

4. List them.

5. Now, laugh at each of them. Go for it—a loud belly laugh.

6. Declare the truth that would counter each of those lies. (Exercise 99 will help you with this step.)

On a Personal Note

I am indebted to my friend Steve Backlund for this strategy. When I learned it from him and practiced it, it felt weird to generate a laugh that wasn't spontaneous. Once I got past the awkwardness of it, it was a blast. To learn more about this read Steve's book: *Let's Just Laugh At That.*[17]

EXERCISES
THAT BRING US
FREEDOM

60

A BEGINNER'S FAST

My nourishment comes from doing the will of God
(John 4:34).

For some of us, skipping a few meals in order to focus on our relationship with God has become a key for spiritual renewal. Fasting for a day, three days, and occasionally three weeks is not uncommon. It can become part of a lifestyle.

If you think it is strange, remember that this discipline was common in the lives of God's people throughout the Bible. In some church streams and cultures Christians fast regularly because they've discovered its power to increase our faith for spiritual breakthroughs. However, you may have grown up in a church culture that has not placed value in fasting. Don't worry, it's never too late to learn!

Here's one way to successfully complete a one day fast (and enjoy it):

1. Pick a twenty-eight hour period in which you have no special meals planned: no lunch, breakfast or dinner appointments. No birthday celebrations or holidays.

2. Enjoy a healthy lunch.

3. Abstain from eating after lunch until the following evening about 6 p.m.

4. Drink plenty of water. If you feel very weak, drink a glass of fruit juice when you would normally eat.

5. Here's the key: Take the time you would be preparing your meal, eating, and cleaning up the dishes **to pray**. Otherwise, it's simply a starvation diet.

6. During each meal time envision offering to God what you would be eating: "Father my food this meal is to do your will." "I offer this simple sacrifice as my gift to you." "I love you more than food." "You are my God, not my stomach."

7. Pray prayers of gratitude, adoration, and surrender during your prayer times. I find my faith for specific needs to be high when I'm fasting. A friend who is sick, a financial need, or wisdom for a decision I'm facing are the kinds of petition prayers I boldly ask for during a fast.

You will find such joy and fulfillment when you reach the finish line and sit down to enjoy that meal. This three-meal fast may even "whet your appetite" for a longer fast of three, five or even 21 days. Such fasts are life changing.

On a Personal Note

I am one of those "live to eat" kind of guys. Food is often far too important to me. I think that's why I often feel the need to fast. I've had the grace to fast for multiple three, five, seven, fourteen and twenty-one day fasts, and even one twenty-eight-day fast. I've never regretted any fast I have done—each one has been much more beneficial than I could ever describe. More things happened in me and through my prayers during those fasts than I could recount in a book. However, I honestly think that the long-term impact of fasting one day a week (like the fast described above) for twenty-one weeks is even more beneficial than twenty-one straight days of fasting.[18]

61

CELEBRATING FREEDOM

*I have the right to do anything, but I will not be
mastered by anything"*
(Apostle Paul in 1 Corinthians 6:12).

The spiritual disciplines are all about freedom. It is easy to find ourselves mastered by certain habits in our lives. Those habits are not necessarily sinful, but over time we can become enslaved by them. Any innocent hobby or pastime can become an obsession. We can begin to find comfort in silly, meaningless activities rather than finding comfort in God.

Here's a simple exercise that can bring a renewed sense of the victory Jesus won through the resurrection.

1. Find a quiet place and time to center your heart on God.

2. When you have freed your mind of clutter, tell the Father you are sincerely wanting to know if anything has begun to take His place as master of your life. "Is there something in my daily schedule that's drawing my affections away from you?" "Please show me where I'm finding comfort rather than your presence." "Am I being mastered by something other than you?"

3. Now trust the Holy Spirit to speak to you. Remember, He doesn't condemn us. He leads us in joyful obedience that brings life.

4. If the Holy Spirit reveals something, write it down (so as not to forget).

5. Now ask Him if there is a length of time that you should lay aside this activity or habit.

6. Be sure and replace that activity with a life-giving spiritual exercise.

On a Personal Note

Once the Holy Spirit showed me that I was spending way too much of my time reading novels. He gave me the grace to put aside novels for a year. During that time of the day (or night) that I would have been lost in a novel, I chose instead to read a good biography, a book focused on Biblical teaching or a book on church history. After a year I picked up an occasional novel without feeling mastered by that hobby. That was 25 years ago.

More recently I found myself playing some dumb games on my iPad just to take my mind off of work and ministry. I would often do this just before I went to sleep. I made a simple decision to replace the time I spent playing games with memorizing Scripture. Which do *you* think is more life-giving?

62

Power to Resist Temptation

It (the grace of God) teaches us to say "No" to ungodliness
and worldly passions, and to live self-controlled,
upright and godly lives in this present age
(Titus 2:12).

Every one of us has places in our lives where we are most vulnerable to sin. It could be a tendency to cycle back to internet pornography or to fly off the handle in rage or blatant selfishness. Just as sinister are heart attitudes like pride, judgment, or a victim mentality. You know what I'm talking about. We call those flesh patterns. When we are not abiding in Christ, we can easily fall back into habits, attitudes, and choices that are more like the life we turned away from to follow Christ than the new life He has for us. Something in us dies when we don't know how to consistently say "no" to those temptations. "The wages of sin is death" (Romans 6:33). We also grieve the Spirit and break God's heart. Every aspect of our destiny and fruitfulness in Him is affected if we are okay just living in this lie of our enemy.

Here's the good news: what Christ did for us through His death not only dealt with our past failures, but also freed us from the power of sin in our lives. The power that raised Jesus from the dead lives in us and is much more powerful than we could ever fully grasp.

This exercise helps to understand that power. It will position us to let the grace of God to do its work in us, empowering us to say NO.

1. Read the following verses: Romans 5:17; 6:1-7, 10-14, 17-18, 22; 7:4-6; 8:1-14; Galatians 2:20; 5:24

2. Now, read them again making a list of statements that declare how we have been freed from the power of sin through the death of Christ.

3. Thank God that this true for every sin pattern that you've repeatedly "fallen into."

4. Ask His forgiveness for believing the lie that you are "bound" to keep committing these familiar (besetting) sins. Acknowledge that you are responsible for the choices that you've made to allow those things that you are *dead* to come back to life.

5. Now in prayer do what we are admonished to do in:

   - Romans 6:11 — "Lord Jesus, I consider myself dead to_____ (list the flesh patterns). I am not defined by those sins, but rather I have a new identity in you." Now pray using your own way of expressing it.

   - Romans 6:12 — "I refuse to let_____ (name those recurring sins) control the way I live." Now pray using your own way of expressing it.

   - Romans 6:13 — "I give you_____ (list the parts of your body previously involved in sin) as instruments of righteousness." Now pray using your own way of expressing it.

   - Romans 8:13 — "By the power of your death and resurrection, I put to death _____ (name the sins you keep repeating). I renounce any involvement in them any longer." Now pray using your own way of expressing it.

- Galatians 5:24 — "I declare that _____ (name the sins you keep repeating) has been nailed to the cross. They are dead and I am dead to them." Now pray using your own way of expressing it.

6. Now personalize Titus 2:11-12. Make it your prayer. Ask the Lord to show you specific ways the grace of God is teaching you to say "no" to ungodliness and unholy passions. Wait on Him and write down what you are hearing.

7. Finally, ask the Lord to show you who might be an accountability partner. Or, with whom you might start a Life Transformation Group (see exercise 77).

On a Personal Note

You may have been taught that the struggle with the sinful nature Paul talks about in Romans 7 is his (and thus our) current personal struggle with sin. That was what I was taught in my early discipleship. That is an erroneous interpretation of that passage. For a right understanding of Romans 7 I strongly recommend Douglas J. Moo's *The Epistle to the Romans: New International Commentary on the New Testament.*

63

THE FREEDOM OF A CLEAN CONSCIENCE

*So I strive always to keep my conscience
clean before God and man*
(Acts 24:16).

A clean conscience is more valuable than a billion dollars. But obtaining and maintaining a clean conscience is no easy task. That is why it involved striving for the Apostle Paul. It's one thing to find forgiveness in simple sincere prayer to Jesus invoking the power of His sacrificial death for us. But notice, Paul said before God and man. When I sin against God by speaking harshly with my spouse I can't simply deal with it by confessing it to God. I must humble myself before my wife and ask her forgiveness. It involves both a vertical and horizontal transaction. And note the challenge of always. I can't be really free with a conscience that's clean only six days a week or one that was clean last week, but not today. The problem is there are often fresh violations of our conscience. We need to stay current.

Out of much practice, I offer you these steps to make it right.

1. Ask the Holy Spirit to show you if there is some way you've wronged someone that you need to go to and make it right

(He usually speaks to us about these before we are asking… He's really good at his job!).

Here are some things the Holy Spirit has brought to my attention in my past:

- a lie I need to confess
- something I need to pay for that I've stolen
- money or things that I've borrowed and not returned
- a promise I've not kept
- a person's character that I defamed
- inappropriate remarks
- deliberately giving an impression that's untrue

2. One way to be aware of the need to "make it right" is if there is anyone who you would feel uncomfortable running into at the supermarket because "you owe them," because there is a conversation (or restitution) that should have taken place but did not.

3. Think through exactly how you wronged the person or people involved.

4. Confess it to God and receive His forgiveness (if you haven't). Do so taking full responsibility for your sinful choice.

5. Ask His help to be bold, honest, and humble.

6. Go for it. Contact them. Confess it. Pay it back. Ask forgiveness. No excuses. Don't bring up any way that they may have wronged you. Own your part fully.

7. Now celebrate the glorious freedom of a squeaky-clean conscience.

On a Personal Note

This is one of the most liberating exercises there is. It is the pathway to inviting God's kingly reign in every relationship. Once you experience the freedom of this kind of lifestyle you never want to hide things or blow off past mistakes. You want to deal with it. There's fresh power to avoid so many sinful choices—to live out the holiness that Jesus works in us. How often I think "I'm not going there because I know I will just have to come clean with if I want to keep enjoying the freedom of integrity I now enjoy."

64

A FAST FROM YOUR ELECTRONIC DEVICES

You may be surprised how many hours of your day you are on your smart phone, sending and receiving text messages, tweeting, checking your Facebook page, or using one of your other favorite apps. Most of us spend a good chunk of our forty-hour work week sitting in front of a computer. Even our discretionary time is usually spent staring at a screen, like a television. What would life be like if we didn't have these distracting devices?

This exercise gives us a taste of that.

1. Select a 48-hour period that works for you. This will probably have to be on a weekend or a holiday for most people.

2. Turn off and put aside every device. Be decisive and ruthless.

3. Use the time spent using these devices (this could be hours in your day!) to nurture your relationship with God and others.

4. Reflect in your prayer journal your experience at the end of those forty-eight hours.

5. If this experience brings grace for you as it has for me you will want to try an even longer period of time: three days or even a week.

On a Personal Note

I often combine a media fast with a food fast or a silent retreat. During my weekly twenty-eight-hour food fast I avoid movies, videos, and television. It's so liberating for me to just take a break from the noise and use as much of my discretionary time as possible connecting with the Lord.

One more time we abstain from our electronic devices as a family is while eating together. Even in restaurants where we live it's rare to see a table where people are engaging in conversation. Everyone is on their hand held devices interacting with social media, texting, or playing games. What a wasted opportunity for life-giving interaction with people we love.

Exercises that Help Us Listen

65

A Silent Retreat

Be still, and know that I am God!
(Psalm 46:10).

Imagine a 48-hour period in which the only sound you hear is the sound of birds, leaves blowing in the wind, or the distant bark of a dog. Is it hard to imagine? You and nearly other human being alive in the 21st century can't relate to such stillness. Televisions, radios, electronic devices, people talking, traffic noise, and a host of other noisy clatter keeps us from obeying this admonition, "Be still, and know that I am God" (Psalm 46:10). Finding or creating this kind of space in one's life takes major intentionality for most of us, but experiencing God in silence and solitude is definitely worth the sacrifice.

Here's how I've done it:

1. Find a place where you can be alone for a weekend. Google "silent retreat" if you don't have friends with a lake house or mountain cabin. Often monasteries or church retreat centers are available for outside guests.

2. Be ruthless in your avoidance of noise-making devices. Let the only human voice you hear for forty-eight hours be that of your own talking or singing to God.

3. Lay aside games, novels, internet, and any other distractions.

4. Leave your computer and tablet at home unless you use them for reading the word or journaling.

5. Read large chunks of your Bible. Take walks out doors. Sleep as much as your body needs. It would be ideal to fast, but if you need to eat, eat only simple meals.

6. Pray and ask the Holy Spirit to lead you to do five to ten of the exercises found in this book during your retreat.

7. Journal what you hear and what you experience.

8. Ask, "Father, what adjustments do I need to make in my life right now to experience more of your resurrection life?"

On a Personal Note

I never regret the time, energy, or expense it takes to un-plug from the *matrix*. I often go with one agenda in mind or a certain goal I want to accomplish, only to find that God has a different plan for our time together. Without exception, as I am heading back home after such a retreat, I think "I really want to schedule more of these."

66

IF GOD WERE
SPEAKING TO ME ...

The God of the Bible is a God who loves to reveal Himself. He's a communicative God. But often we His people experience Him as being silent. Perhaps that's why most of our interaction with God is us doing all the talking. We need to cultivate a listening heart.

This exercise helps us learn to hear God.

1. Find a comfortable sitting position in a room that is quiet where you are alone.

2. Take ten to twenty minutes and express your sincere gratitude and adoration for God.

3. Now in your prayer journal or on a piece of paper write: "If God were speaking to me today He would say:_____" (I use red ink here.)

4. Write what comes to mind. Don't second guess what you're hearing. Don't fear "making this up." Just write out impressions of what the Father is speaking to you in first person in this moment.

5. Now respond to Him according to what you heard.

6. If what you heard is weird or condemning, submit it to your spouse or some other trusted friend in your Christian community for feedback.

On a Personal Note

Honestly, the clearest, most profound things I hear from God come to me at times I least expect it. He speaks 'out of the blue,' so to speak, rather than when I have pen and prayer journal in hand. But when I still my soul and ask: "If you were speaking to me right now, what would you be saying?" there's almost always an impression. I have noticed that most of what I hear has one of four themes:

1. His personal love and affirmation of me.

2. His encouragement for me to trust Him. "Quit worrying."

3. "Go for it, I am with you." "Step out in faith." "Don't be afraid."

4. "Quit taking yourself so seriously."

67

DISCERNING GOD'S COUNSEL

*You are controlled by the Spirit if you have the Spirit of God
living in you. (And remember that those who do not have the
Spirit of Christ living in them do not belong to Him at all)*
(Romans 8: 9).

We all experience situations where we need to make a decision and we wish that God would just give us a really clear sign from heaven. But at times, God seems silent. We know that He has given us His Spirit to lead us and give us wisdom, but it's often not easy for us to *hear what He's saying*. This exercise will help you discern the Spirit's intimate counsel so you can make better decisions. But first there are basic assumptions about our hearts that you need to believe.

- The first is based on the above passage in Romans 8:9—God's Spirit is in us leading us to do the right thing.

- Secondly, from the same chapter, verse 15, it says that the Spirit helps us relate to God as *Abba* (Daddy). We can "cry out to Him" for His counsel and He's eager to give it. (For those of us who are parents this makes total sense.)

- As His children, we are being led by the Spirit to please Him (see verse 5).

- That leadership results in life and peace (see verse 6).

I think Ignatius got it right. "God, through His Spirit is present in the deepest core of our being," he said. "Thus we can discern the will of God in our deepest desires." The goal is to "sort through our superficial and fleeting desires and tap into deep, holy longings. God's desires for us and our deepest desires are, in the end, not opposed but are one and the same."[19]

With this bedrock belief …

1. Write down (or type out) exactly what the decision is that you are facing.

2. Honestly express your own inability to discern what's best in the decision you are facing. Feel free to ask Him why He has seemed so silent up until now.

3. Now read Romans 8 and highlight every verse that speaks to God's help in this decision. Turn these verses into personal declarations of trust in His Spirit's help.

4. Ask yourself the following questions and ask the Spirit to help you be completely honest (He is, after all, the Spirit of Truth).

   • What are the advantages and disadvantages of making choice A and B?

   • What are my true motives for each course of action?

   • What advice would I give someone else considering this same choice?

   • Which choice do I want to be part of the story I tell to my kids and grandkids some day?

   • Imagine standing before the Lord (and we all will) and talking through what the decision you've made. Which does He seem to be smiling on?

5. If you were to give a percentage value of which choice, A or B, which has the higher score? What do you want most

in your heart of hearts after asking yourself the previous questions? If one is stronger …

6. Try it on. Act as if you have made the choice without telling anyone else your final decision for three days. Does it feel peaceful? God's peace will not prevail if you are making the wrong choice.

7. Don't make a final decision until you have to. Take a day or three to fast (the bigger the decision, the longer the fast). Invite counsel from trusted friends and mentors. If you are married, go through this whole process with your spouse.

8. Make your decision with great confidence and joy, knowing God will redirect you if He has a better plan.

On a Personal Note

I could give several personal examples of huge life decisions where I went through the process listed above and still felt a measure of doubt and confusion. I don't think I have ever been even 80 percent sure about any decision except the one to marry Janine. But I do not regret any of these decisions now. God led. In one major decision, I thought I perceived God's will and after announcing my choice, God made it really clear to me within twenty-four hours that I had made the wrong choice. I reversed my decision. It was so embarrassing to backtrack and undo several conversations. But that experience gave me assurance that if we are sincere, the Spirit won't allow us to make the wrong choice.

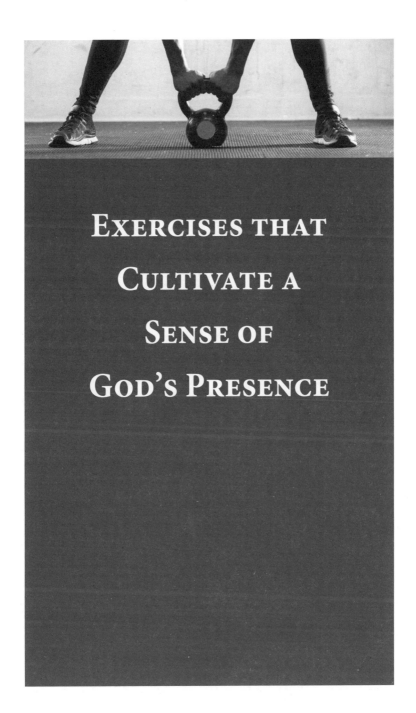

Exercises that Cultivate a Sense of God's Presence

68

A MIND FIXED
ON CHRIST

Set your minds on things above, not on earthly things.
For you died, and your life is now hidden with Christ in God
(Colossians 3:2-3).

Frank Laubach was best known for developing a literary program while living among Muslims in the Philippians in the 1930's that was eventually used to teach over 60 million people around the world to read. The impact he has had on me and many others was his commitment to live every moment of his life aware the presence of God.

Fixing his mind on Christ became his passion. He developed what he called the "Game of Minutes." He called it a game because he wanted it to be light-hearted and he found it to be "a delightful experience and an exhilarating spiritual exercise."

Here's how it goes:

1. Set aside an hour without other commitments or distractions. Laubach called it an "uncomplicated hour." It may be an hour of a boring task in which your mind has little else to do. It could be during a task like commuting in a car alone, working out, waiting for a delayed flight, et cetera.

2. During this hour think about Jesus at least once every minute. Consider His attributes. Think about His responses to people. Recount the stories from the Gospels. Imagine His countenance. Dwell on names He or others used for Him.

3. At the end of the hour, be honest about your experience. Was it life-giving? Delightful? Or was it an exercise in futility because your mind kept wandering? Listen to Frank Laubach's encouraging words: "You may not win all of your minutes to Christ, or even half, but you do win a richer life. There are no losers except those who quit." [20]

On a Personal Note

Outside of the first hour or two every morning I find thinking about Jesus every minute of an hour after that really challenging. I can easily converse with Him or even talk about Him for an hour. I can praise Him or thank Him for an hour, but just going there in my thoughts ... this is a stretch. Help! Just being honest.

69

A Running Conversation with God

Pray continually
(1 Thessalonians 5:17).

Frank Laubach found one way to live out this admonition was to invite God into the internal conversation going on inside our heads. "My part is to live this hour in continual conversation with God and in perfect responsiveness to His will, to make this hour gloriously rich."[21] Do you see the difference between this and the above exercise? That one is about focused thoughts. This one is a conversation.

Here's a way to practice this discipline:

1. Pick an hour that you will be alone. Pick a place you can talk out loud without someone thinking you are crazy.

2. Now begin to monitor the stream of consciousness going on in your mind. Turn every idea you are "mulling over" into a conversation with God (or Christ). Have a dialog with Him about every thought. For example: "Lord, I'm not feeling very excited about this latest project my boss has dropped in my lap. What's your thought about this? Is it time to send out my resume? You know I've been looking for a good reason to get out of this job. What's your counsel …?" In one hour you may have forty different ideas stream through. Try to "take captive" every one of them.

3. At the end of the hour, try to evaluate your experience. Did you feel God's presence more than usual? Was it challenging? What could you do differently in order to really carry on a continual conversation for an hour?

4. When you feel that you have mastered that "uncomplicated hour" of conversation with God, try it when you are in the middle of a busy work day. Frank Laubach found it to be possible: "You do not need to forget other things or stop your work, but invite Him to share everything you do or say or think. . . ."

On a Personal Note

Although this exercise was easier for me than the previous one. I still feel like a spiritual midget when I think how far I am from having these kinds of hour-long *Laubach conversations* with God throughout the day. Our conversations are often one-sided. I'm doing all the talking. I love Laubach's challenge to *invite Him to share everything you do or say or think*. I feel encouraged to grow in engaging the Father in these kinds of dialog.

70

Practicing
His Presence

All of us want to cultivate a sense of God's presence throughout our day. I know very few Christians who have mastered this as a lifestyle. Most feel challenged in just developing a consistent quiet time in the mornings.

The following exercise is designed to help us keep turning our hearts back to God in a persistent manner throughout our day.

1. Set you watch alarm or cell phone alarm to go off once every hour from the time you normally get up to the last hour of your day.

2. When your alarm sounds, take three minutes to interact with God (yes, only 180 seconds). For the first minute, center your thoughts on God. Think of His attributes, His names, mental images of God that are true to His character. Adore Him for who He is.

3. After one minute of letting your thoughts be focused on Him, thank Him for ways He has loved you, blessed you and answered your prayers. Do this for one minute.

4. In the third and final minute of your hourly pause, pray a prayer of surrender. "Father, I give myself to you." "My life is yours." "You are the boss and you are in charge." You get the idea.

5. After about three minutes, go about the routines and work of your day.

On a Personal Note

I, along with many people in my church, tried this for a week. I was so aware of changes taking place in me, of actually abiding in His presence more than usual, that I re-upped for three more weeks. I know some of you are saying; "I've got a job," or "I've got a class that I'm teaching," or "I'm caring for a patient or children," et cetera. "How can I just drop all that and pray?" Even with these challenges you can find a way to do this if you are motivated. I remember being in the middle of meetings I was leading and I just took a bathroom break and whispered out my three minute prayer in the stall! A couple of hundred other people that took the challenge would attest to similar experiences to mine during that week. Try it.

71

THE DAILY OFFICE

This exercise dates back sixteen centuries and is practiced, with some minor variations, by various Catholic and Orthodox monastic orders until today. Many of us Evangelicals are currently exploring the treasure of monastic spirituality. If that's you, this exercise is a must. It is also called *fixed hour prayer, Divine Office,* or *liturgy of the hours.* The word *Office* comes from the Latin word *opus* or "work." A quick look at the fixed times of prayers makes it easy to see why it is called the work of God. There are seven of them inspired by David in Psalm 119:164. The times are 3:45 a.m., 6:00 a.m., 6:25 a.m., 12:15 p.m., 2:00 p.m., 5:40 p.m., and 7:40 p.m.

These prayer times become fixed points in our daily schedule during which we press the pause button of our busy lives and *be with* God.

The prayer times can be as short or as long as you want but they have four basic elements:

1. You stop what you are doing.
2. Centering. This is similar to what many of the other spiritual exercises require:
   - Sitting still in a comfortable position
   - Slowing your breathing
   - Closing your eyes
   - Focusing your thoughts
   - Being attentive to God's presence

3. Silence

4. Scripture

For seasoned practitioners of the Daily Office, the Psalms are essential. They pray or sing through all 150 every week. Other Old and New Testament readings can be integrated. You can turn the Scripture readings into personal prayers (like exercises _____). You can meditate on verses. You can play and sing along with worship music. You can pray prayers of gratitude, adoration, surrender, repentance and trust. You can read from devotional books. There's flexibility. I love what Peter Scazzero says: "If it helps, do it. If it doesn't help you, don't do it…. The purpose of the Daily Office is to remember God and commune with Him all through our days." Peter Scazzero has much more to say about this practice in his book: *Emotionally Healthy Spirituality: It's Impossible to Be Spiritually Mature, While Remaining Emotionally Immature.*

On a Personal Note

I have known about the Daily Office for years, but the 3:45 a.m. wake-up call has made me less than enthusiastic about following this set schedule. The fact that 100's of thousands monks and nuns have found something life-giving in this schedule of daily prayer over the last 1600 years motivated me to give it try. I found it rather restricting. The 3:45 a.m. was a bust—my prayers were incoherent, lame at best. The 6:00 a.m. bled into 7:00 a.m. Let me say it this way: I think there are personality types that thrive on this kind of ordering of one's devotional schedule. I am not one.

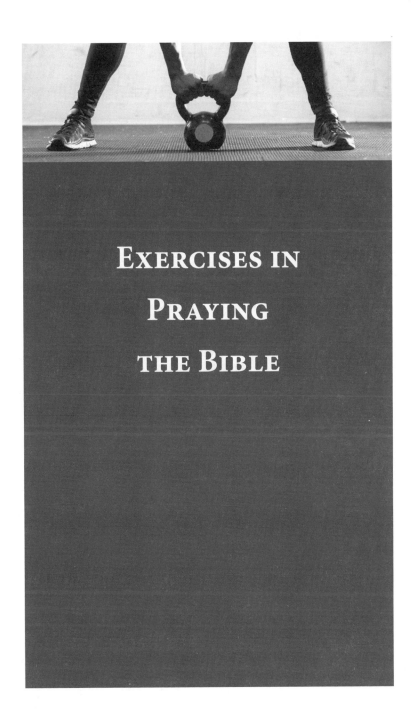

EXERCISES IN PRAYING THE BIBLE

72

PRAYERS OF
THE BIBLE

Perhaps the easiest way to pray using the Bible is to pray prayers found in the Bible. There are hundreds...more than 175 in the New Testament alone! Many of the Psalms are essentially prayers put to music. Herbert Lokyer has provided an incredible resource for praying biblical prayers. He has not only identified the passages that are prayers, he has summarized for us the topic of each prayer. Go to www.lbdsoftware.com/All%20the%20Prayers%20of%20the%20Bible.pdf to see this extensive list.

1. Using Lokyer's list, pick out a prayer from the Old Testament that seems relevant to your situation and read it out loud.

2. Now personalize it.

3. Do the same for one of the New Testament prayers.

4. Repeat this exercise, praying as many of these prayers as possible.

5. When you come across prayers that are particularly meaningful to you, copy and paste them into a file for future use.

6. Memorizing these prayers for spontaneous use will prove to be powerful "prayer fodder."

On a Personal Note

I've learned so much about prayer through praying these prayers. My faith soars as I personalize the heart cries of Daniel, David, Moses, Isaiah, Paul, and the other heroes of faith in the Bible.

73

KNOWING GOD THROUGH JESUS

The Son is the image of the invisible God. . .
(Colossians 1:20)

When you've seen me, you've seen the Father
(John 14:12)

People in every religion grapple with the question of God. "What is God really like?" Thousands of volumes have been written just by Christian theologians trying to dissect and systematize the nature of God, His character and His person (not to mention other world religions).

The following exercise takes us straight to the source: Jesus.

1. Pick one of the four Gospels: Matthew, Mark, Luke, or John.

2. Read carefully every verse in every chapter with this question in mind: "What do we learn about God from Jesus?" Not just what Jesus said, but His attitudes and actions.

3. Try just three or four chapters a day and you will get through one of the Gospels in a week.

4. Take notes in your prayer journal and then declare them out loud to God in awe and gratitude.

You may be surprised at what new things you discover about God through this exercise.

On a Personal Note

Trying this through the book of Mark recently, I was struck at how often God (through Jesus) shows His love for the least of these: the humble, the lowly, the weak and the hurting. God also seems to be eager to call people to Himself so that He can send them out to help others. In chapters six through nine of the Gospel of Mark, it is obvious that God does not like demons. He likes to send them away, drive them out (through Jesus). He's okay with people other than the twelve casting out demons in His name and disappointed when the disciples themselves don't have the faith to do so. That's an example of something that stood out to me. I love this exercise!

74

BIBLE IMMERSION

Your word is a lamp for my feet, a light on my path
(Psalm 119:105).

Most of us have attempted reading the Bible through in a year. What about reading the Bible through every twenty-eight days? It is possible. I have a friend and former missionary colleague named John (Bud) Brown who practiced this disciple for decades. Yes, he read the Bible through over one hundred times!

Here's how he did it:

1. Count the number of pages in your Bible and divide by twenty-eight. (Don't do it by chapters because the length of chapters vary.)

2. Day 1: Read at your normal pace and see how long it takes to get through your daily reading. This would be 1/28ᵗʰ of the Bible. Block out that amount of time each day for the next twenty-seven days.

3. It's a bit more complicated, but if you can divide the Old Testament pages by twenty-eight and then do the same for the New Testament, you can get a dose of both the Old and New Testaments every day.

4. Take note of at least one new inspiring insight or new idea from every reading.

5. If you have a long commute or work a job that allows you to listen to audio recordings, use an audio Bible.

On a Personal Note

I've never read the Bible in a month, but I do know the value of reading all the way through in less than a year (at least nine times and counting). Here are some of the benefits: You get the 30,000-feet altitude view. You see the big picture of God's redemptive plan. It's like inheriting a 10,000-acre ranch and flying over it with a helicopter. You can explore every acre on foot at some point but it's good to see what you have first. It may be something you try once and then go back to the slower pace of dividing the Bible up into 365 portions.

I asked Bud once, "Doesn't it get boring? Reading the Bible over and over like that?" His response was: "No, it's like a daily commute through a beautiful countryside. The familiarity evokes affection. And there's always something new. Every day you notice some other beautiful sight you've never seen before."

75

Bible Reading
into Prayer

*God uses it (Scripture) to prepare and equip
His people to do every good work
(2 Timothy 3:17).*

This following process can be applied to whatever you are reading in the Bible. Even one of the "drier" chapters in Leviticus can become a source of rich fodder to be used in prayer.

1. Read the chapter in your daily reading. You may have a chapter from the New Testament, one from the Psalms, and a couple from the Old Testament. Select one to start with that you will use to develop this skill.

2. Read the chapter carefully a second time, looking for something about God or Jesus for which you can praise Him. Create prayers of adoration that are expressed directly from God's Word. Take a moment to say the prayers out loud to God as an expression of your heart.

3. Now note something from this chapter for which you are thankful. Pray a specific prayer of gratitude incorporating the verse(s) from this chapter.

4. Repeat this process if there's something you find that brings conviction: something that you are *not* doing, something

you need to stop doing or anything you need to confess or repent of. Voice it as a sincere prayer.

5. Perhaps something you read in this chapter kindles a request or longing in your heart. Pray a prayer of petition that comes from the truth of these verses.

6. Is there something that the Spirit is highlighting for you to obey? Commit yourself to obedience in a prayer.

You will find that when you engage the Word through praying it, its impact will be phenomenal. When you pray Scripture it becomes etched in our thoughts and spirit. God's Spirit transforms us through this process.

* If you read your Bible using Kindle you can make notes by simply clicking the sentence then adding your prayer. On your next reading of the text you can pull up your previous prayer and pray it again.

On a Personal Note

I have read and prayed through the Bible this way a number of times. Every time I do, I'm amazed at how much bigger God seems. Each time I find so many more prayers of adoration, thanksgiving confession, and surrender to pray. I believe that if I were to read the Bible a thousand times, I would still find fresh prayers to pray.

76

TAKING PART IN THE NARRATIVE

As Jesus approached Jericho,
a blind beggar was sitting beside the road
(Luke 18:35).

Have you ever read the narratives in the New Testament and wished you could have been there to witness in person that event? With the help of the Holy Spirit and your God-given imagination, you can experience the story.

Here is a simple way in which you can put yourself into the narrative and have it become more real to you.

1. Pick one of your favorite stories from the Bible. Read it out loud. For example, one of mine is the story of Jesus healing the blind beggar on the road approaching Jericho, found in Luke 18: 35-43.

2. Now, focus on one of the characters in the narrative. Let's start with the beggar. Imagine yourself as the beggar. Close your eyes. Pretend that you are this man in the position he is in. There is no hope for you to see again, but because you have heard of the miracles of Jesus you dare to have hope that He could perform a miracle and make you see. Play act his part in the story. Cry out in desperation: "Jesus, Son of David, have mercy on me!" Get into the role. Use the same tone and volume he must have used.

3. Ask yourself "how do I feel?" "What would I have done differently?" "How would I react to all of the people telling me to be quiet?" Finally, ask "what would it be like to begin to see after Jesus healed me?" Maybe you would imagine a feeling of gratitude, awe and adoration.

4. Now express these feelings to Jesus in prayer. Have we not all been made to see spiritually in an equally dramatic manner?

5. Now place yourself in the crowd telling the beggar to be quiet. Go through the same questions. Be honest with yourself. What would I have done differently? Think about the change that took place in them after the healing.

6. Now place yourself in the role of Jesus. Imagine what could have He felt. Envision the power of God working through you in that manner.

7. Pray whatever prayers of repentance, petition, submission, or adoration that come to mind..

On a Personal Note

For seasoned Bible readers, this is one way to help these familiar stories take on new life.

77

LIFE TRANSFORMATION GROUPS

Unlike ninety-eight of the other spiritual exercises in this book, this one requires at least one other person, preferably two. A Life Transformation Group consists of three people lovingly holding each other accountable for spiritual growth. There are two elements to experiencing the power of this discipline. The first takes place between weekly meetings. It involves an agreed upon reading of a portion of Scripture every week. Select twenty-five to thirty chapters. If, for example, you pick a shorter book like Ephesians, then read the whole book each day. If Corinthians, then agree to read half of it each day. If it's a longer book like Acts, Revelation, or one of the gospels, then read it together once that week. It's important for the group to weigh in and be fully involved in the decision about what you will read.

The second important element is the meeting itself. For obvious reasons the group needs to be with trusted friends of the same gender. The ideal size is three people. The meeting involves accountability questions in an atmosphere of love and support.

Here are ten questions that you can choose from:

1. Have you been a testimony this week to the greatness of Jesus Christ with both your words and actions?

2. Have you been exposed to sexually alluring material or allowed your mind to entertain inappropriate sexual thoughts about another person this week?

3. Have you lacked any integrity in any of your financial dealings this week, or coveted something that doesn't belong to you?

4. Have you been honoring, understanding, and generous in all of your important relationships this past week?

5. Have you damaged another person by your words, either behind his/her back or face-to-face?

6. Have you given in to an addictive behavior this week? Explain.

7. Have you continued to remain angry toward someone?

8. Have you secretly wished for another's misfortune that you might excel?

9. Did you finish your Bible reading this week? What did you hear? What are you going to do about it?

10. Have you been completely honest with us?

Taking time in your meeting for loving exhortation, affirmation and prayer is vital.

On a Personal Note

I took this directly from Neil Cole's Book's *Cultivating a Life for God*.[22] We encouraged everyone in our church to be involved in one of these transformational groups during the first three years of our church plant. The combination of reading large chunks of Scripture and the accountability questions have helped so many grow up spiritually. After three years we began to personalize the accountability questions to our unique temptations. This has been so helpful.

78

MEDITATING ON SCRIPTURE

One verse

S tudy this Book of Instruction continually. Meditate on it day and night so you will be sure to obey everything written in it. Only then will you prosper and succeed in all you do (Joshua 1:8).

1. Pick one of your favorite verses in the Bible. If you have not yet done so, commit it to memory. This way you can pull up the verse wherever you are throughout the day.

2. Now take each part of the passage and dissect its meaning. For example, one of my favorite passages is Philippians 4:19: "And my God will supply all your needs according to His riches in glory in Christ Jesus." I start with "My God."

3. Quote the verse with an emphasis on these first two words. Repeat it several times. As I reflect on these two words, ideas come to mind like: He's my **God**. He's personal. He's my father. He is my God. I may think about names and character traits of God. You get the picture.

4. Now take the next phrase, "will meet of all of your needs." "Will" speaks of certainty. What are synonyms for "meet"? Does all mean **all**? As I turn these thoughts into prayers for specific needs in my life, faith arises in my heart.

To use a rather homey illustration I heard years ago, this meditation process is much like a cow digesting its food. It has three stomachs. There's the initial ingestion of freshly eaten grass. Then in moving from one stomach to the next, the grass is broken down further and further until it's fully and completely ingested. In a similar way, we fully absorb the Word of God when we digest it in waves of prayerful meditation.

On a Personal Note

Going over and over a verse in my thoughts, focusing on each word, makes the meaning of the verse come alive for me. Imagine if you and I picked only one verse a week and memorized it, then meditated on the verse three times at thirty minutes per session the next week. The impact would be incredible! And for a guy my age, I would have more than 1,092 verses imbedded in my soul because I started doing this activity at a pace much faster than one verse a week from the time I was nineteen years of age!

79

MEMORIZING AND MEDITATING ON SCRIPTURE

Large Chunks

Every Christian wishes they had large portions of Scripture committed to memory. Even if we have never done it, we could all recite the benefits hiding God's Word in our hearts. But the time commitment and amount of effort required to memorize large portions of Scripture is daunting.

Here is one motivation (among several) that makes it worth it. Memorizing large chunks of Scripture can be a deeply spiritual experience. Andrew Davis points out that Jesus spoke of the power of the Word that happens in heart transformation: "However, the Word of God must enter us through our MIND—through our understanding—in order to change our hearts. Thus we are to meditate deeply on Scripture in order to understand it better, so that our hearts may be changed. And we are to meditate on every word that comes from the mouth of God. There is no more useful discipline to this careful process of verse by verse meditation than memorization. Memorization is not the same as meditation, but it is almost impossible for someone to memorize a passage of Scripture without somewhat deepening his/her understanding of those verses."[23]

Here are some keys to turning this discipline into a lifestyle of filling your mind with spiritual truth:

1. Prayerfully choose a favorite chapter from the Bible. (Romans 8, 12, Ephesians 1,3,6, Colossians 1,3, Matthew 5-7, Psalm 139 are all popular options).

2. Set memory goals. How many verses will I memorize per week? How long will you work on it per day? When will I have committed it memory such that I can quote it all word for word anywhere, anytime?

3. Memorize the verse numbers, for example: twelve-one, twelve-two, etc.

4. Always review previous verses before you start on a new one.

5. Repetition over time is key. "Saying a verse one hundred times in one day is not as helpful as saying it every day for one hundred days."[24]

6. Say it out loud.

7. Turn what you are quoting into a prayer of adoration, gratitude, surrender, declaration, or repentance. Interact with God about this truth.

8. Once you've been successful with a chapter, try a whole book.

On a Personal Note

I took on my first whole book at the age of sixty—Ephesians, in both English and Indonesian. It's been a much slower process at this age. Nearly two years into it and I am still not finished, but it is so worth the work. Recalling the verses throughout the day is so powerful for prayer and fixing my thoughts on truth. The goal is not merely memorizing, but is also about what you do with the verses, chapters, and books after memorization. But you can't bypass the memory work. The key is persistent plodding—getting one verse at a time committed to memory while not forgetting the previous verses.

80

Praying Acts

This went on for two years, so that all the Jews and Greeks who lived in the province of Asia heard the word of the Lord (Acts 19:10).

When you read the book of Acts, don't you wish you could have been part of those emerging Christian communities of the first century? Where people were so radically committed to each other they sold their stuff and shared their wealth with other believers in need? Maybe we don't wish to be included when the Christians were persecuted, but what about when people with major disabilities were radically healed through a simple prayer or command? Where "the Lord was adding to their number daily those being saved" (Acts 2:47)? And on special occasions, when thousands repented and turned to Christ? Or as in the verse above, the gospel spread so rapidly that millions heard in just two years. We can turn those longings into prayers for our church, our community, even places in our world that are as spiritually bankrupt as the Roman Empire was in the first century.

Here's how.

1. Read through the book of Acts on a computer or tablet.

2. Copy and paste your favorite verses or stories into a separate document. You will want to take a key verse or two and not every verse of the narrative. Take special note of Luke's summary statements about the growth and vitality

of those early communities (Acts 2:42-47; 4:32-35; 5:14; 6:7; 8:4; 9:31; 12:24, etc).

3. Create a document that becomes "prayer fodder" based on Acts.

4. Turn these historic statements from the first century church into personalized prayers for your church and community. For example: *"So the message about the Lord spread widely and had a powerful effect"* (Acts 19:20). Turn that into a prayer like, "Lord, may your message of the Good News of the Kingdom spread *in your city or region* and have a powerful effect ..."

5. Pray those prayers for the large unreached people groups of Muslims, Hindus, and Buddhist in other nations.

On a Personal Note

I give a significant amount of my time, and energy researching methods and strategies for church planting movements. At the moment, it's my favorite topic and I interact a lot with others in my field debating and analyzing best practices that can be used so that we will see many new Jesus followers among the unreached. But nothing compares to the book of Acts. It is the original blueprint for disciple-making movements. Talk about powerful, authoritative prayers that reflect the heart of God! I often lead groups in prayers from Acts: our church planting team, workers we are training, churches, or others. More significantly, I personally stay focused on God's goals for the people I'm reaching out to when I pray these prayers.

IGNITING
PASSION IN
PRAYER

81

PRAYING WITH

DIVINE PASSION

*The earnest prayer of a righteous person
produces wonderful results*
(James 5:16).

If you grew up in a predominantly white, evangelical, high church, or denominational church in North American, you probably experienced prayer that wouldn't necessarily be characterized as passionate. This is not a judgment statement about the sincerity or the effectiveness of anyone's prayers. We're talking about a prayer style. Most western Caucasian Christians tend to be more conversational, rational and calm. You notice the contrast if you visit churches that are more racially diverse or if you travel to many parts of Latin America, Africa or Asia. The churches you are likely to encounter in the developing world are ones where people tend to pray loud, passionate prayers and, on occasion, pray all at once. This spiritual exercise will help you pray more like our brothers and sisters who have learned to pray with more intensity and emotion than many of us.

If this type of praying makes you uncomfortable, let me point out the Greek words James uses in the verse noted at the beginning of this exercise: "The earnest (*energeo*) prayer of a righteous person produces (*energeo*) wonderful results."

It's easy to see what English word we get from *energeo*. James is saying: "energized prayer... energizes wonderful results."

Allow the Holy Spirit to move you out of your comfort zone for this experience of praying with more energy and passion than you are used to.

1. Let's start with some "energized" prayers of adoration. Pull out your list of names or adjectives that describe God (from exercise 14). We want to praise the Father (or the Son), not in a low key, conversational, calm manner, but rather with passion. It might help to imagine yourself on the front row of parade in which the float passing right in front of you has your favorite athlete, war hero, celebrity, or rock star. But the difference is that the object of our praise in this case is Jesus! Use the intensity, the volume, and the posture you would exhibit at a parade (you may want to be home alone for this).

2. Now let's petition the Lord with zeal and passion. Bring some of the longings of your heart to the Lord with the intensity of a man trying to wake up his neighbor to borrow some food for an unexpected guest (Luke 11:5-6). Imagine the passion of the woman who approaches the judge day after day and says "Give me justice in this dispute with my enemy" (Luke 18:3). State your petition like she did hers. (It must had some level of energy so as to wear him down!)

3. When you are done, evaluate this experience. Did it feel fake, silly, or unnatural to you? Did it increase your faith level? Your sense of God's presence?

I will give one more encouragement about learning to pray this way: we want to be like Jesus, right? We want to pray like He did? Hebrews says, "During the days of Jesus' life on earth,

He offered up prayers and petitions with fervent cries and tears to the one who could save Him from death" (Hebrews 5:7).

On a Personal Note

When I was a young missionary I would often travel to villages to visit small church plants made up of a small groups of brand new disciples led by Bible School students between nineteen to twenty-two years of age. The congregations were often comprised predominately of subsistence farmers and their families. These were Javanese people who, as a culture, are soft spoken, humble, mild mannered, and extremely subdued in their mannerisms. But when these Jesus loving disciples began to worship and offer themselves to God, it quickly became loud! There was shouting, weeping, laughter, and hands raised to heaven. Talk about passion. I'm sure there was an element of church worship style that they had learned. But I am confident that there was also a deep level appreciation of their new found faith along with a desperation for God for their daily rice.

82

KOREAN-STYLE PRAYER

*When they heard this, they raised their
voices together in prayer to God*
(Acts 4:24).

Praying out loud, together, is often called "Korean-style prayer." However, long before the Korean church came into existence, believers were praying this way (note Acts 4:24). Serial prayers, where we each take turns praying one after the other, is not the only way to pray. There are a lot of non-westerners (besides Koreans) who pray all together.

Obviously, there are occasions where it is appropriate for one individual to lead out in prayer, but many modern Evangelicals know only the one-at-a-time praying method when in a group. It's time to stretch our prayer experiences.

The following is a prayer exercise you can't do alone. Gather some trusted friends or your family. Better yet, suggest it to your small group community.

1. Give time for each person to make a thankful list (see Exercise two).

2. Now, stand together and begin to read your lists out loud as prayers to God together, at the same time. Keep it short, about three minutes.

3. Now talk about it. How did it feel?

4. Try this same kind of prayer together, praying prayers of adoration and praise, once again encouraging a chorus of voices lifted to God.

5. Now pray for individual needs that each person has brought to the gathering, but rather than one person praying, have everyone pray for the same need at the same time. Then shift to the next need. Keep it short.

6. Once again, talk about the experience.

For some it may seem a bit chaotic or confusing, but remember, God is not confused. He can hear us pray all at once. There are benefits to hearing each other's prayers, but too often those who are not praying are not really engaging in prayer while only one person is praying. Our thoughts are floating hither and yon. A combination works well. We can experience the best of both. After the group prays out loud together, have a couple of people re-pray their best prayers while others listen and agree.

On a Personal Note

For those of us who are used to Acts-style prayer, the serial prayer style can honestly seem rather dull and lifeless. On numerous occasions I have introduced the above exercise to people who were not familiar with this style of prayer. Responses have been overwhelmingly positive. A comment I hear often is: "Wow, I was engaged in that prayer so much more than just hearing one person pray."

83

Kingdom of God COME, Will of God BE DONE

Many of us grew up reciting the Lord's Prayer. The tone of it was similar to quoting "Mary had a little lamb…" which is not very convincing or emphatic. But in the original language the verbs used are in the command form. The way Jesus taught His disciples to pray this was more than a hopeful wish or a wimpy plea. It was more like when Gandalf was slamming down his staff and telling Balrog, "You shall not pass."[25] It was authoritative. In reality we have been given the authority to invite or even command God's kingly rule in every realm of our existence.

This may be new to you but you must try it.

1. What is something happening in your life or the life of someone you know and love that is obviously not God's will? If God's will was happening in every human situation, we wouldn't be asked to pray for it to happen—God would just do it without us. Here are some examples:

   - Someone is contemplating walking away from his or her marriage because he or she is drawn into an adulterous relationship;
   - A friend is getting caught up in a cult;
   - Someone is suffering from a chronic illness (there is no illness in heaven);

- Someone desperately needs a job;
- A friend is struggling with drug or alcohol abuse;
- Someone is experiencing depression;
- Someone is dealing with an eating disorder;
- Someone is about to make a rash or foolish choice.

2. Now pray (in an authoritative tone) "Kingdom of God, COME. Will of God BE DONE in _____." Pray as if you are telling the Belrog "You shall not pass!" Expound on what you believe to be God's will for that person. Pray the Scripture. Pray God's promises.

3. You can invite God's kingly authority in many spheres. Here are a few:

   - Your relationships: marriage, parents. children, friends, community. Pray for the Kingdom to come especially in the relationships that are in need of reconciliation or healing.

   - Your church and Christian community. Your pastor and other leaders. You have a sense of what God wants. Go for it in prayer, asking for it to happen.

   - Your neighborhood, city, and nation. Invite the Kingdom in the life and work of every government leader that you can think of. Pray for peace in the key troubled spots of our planet.

   - Your work. Your co-workers.

This kind of prayer is battle, a true spiritual warfare. In your prayers, you may need to address Satan and his wicked hordes. Our enemy is wreaking havoc in so many realms of our existence. As you pray, realize that you are countering his work which is to kill, steal, and destroy.

One way to pray this way is to imagine Jesus standing at the door of your home, church, office or at the front door of the house of someone you are praying for. If you are praying for your neighborhood. city or government on any level this would work. Now open the door and take Jesus by the hand, welcoming Him into the realm you are concerned about. For example, if it's your home, lead Him in and walk Him through each part of your home. Give Him authority in each room and especially in the lives of each of your family members. Invite Him to lead the discussions around the dining table, the interaction in the living room and the fun times in the back yard. You and I have the authority to invite His kingly reign in every realm of our existence.[26]

On a Personal Note

I feel so indebted to my Indonesian friends who follow Jesus and from whom I have learned so much about praying with Kingdom authority. They seem to understand the unseen world of supernatural powers so much more than we westerners. One of many examples: My friend Eddy who pastors a very large church in Jakarta once spoke at a conference we hosted in Austin, Texas. When in the home of one of our pastors he learned that one of that pastor's children, John Mark, was having nightmares. Eddy walked into the child's bedroom and rebuked and banished with Christ's authority the spirits bothering him in the night. Done deal! No more night terrors for John Mark.

84

PRAYERS THAT EXERCISE AUTHORITY

He listened to Paul as he was speaking. Paul looked directly at
him, saw that he had faith to be healed and called out,
"Stand up on your feet!"
At that, the man jumped up and began to walk
(Acts 14:9-10).

Have you ever noticed how many the times Jesus and the early followers of Jesus did not pray when they healed people? They simply commanded or declared a sick or demonized person to be healed and it happened. Jesus and His disciples undoubtedly prayed before these encounters. It's just that the healing or deliverance came as a result of a faith-filled declaration, not a "let's bow our heads and pray" moment.

Occasionally, I stop and boldly pray out loud for someone I've just met who has a need for healing. I have yet to *command* or pronounce healing for someone in Jesus name. I am challenged by the examples in the Gospels and Acts.

Let's try this:

1. Read carefully Matthew 8:16; Mark 9:25; John 5:7-8; Acts 9:34, 14:8-10. What is common about each of these? Can you think of other occasions when people were healed or set free through a simple, authoritative command?

2. Now read Ephesians 1:19; Matthew 18:18; 28:18,20; John 14:12. Ask the Lord to help you see and believe how much authority HE has entrusted to us to minister to people in need.

3. Think of people or situations that you have been praying for that have yet to change. For example: a lingering illness, an emotional or psychological disorder, ongoing abusive behavior, someone who has suicidal thoughts or ongoing self-destructive behavior.

4. Now, after praying to the Father again for that situation, try commanding what you believe to be God's will for them. Imagine yourself talking to the person and declaring them healed or set free. **Unless you've had training and experience in exercising this kind of authority try this at a distance first, not in person.** Say to the person in your imaginary prayer with a lingering leg injury: "Get up and walk freely now." Or to the person dealing with suicidal depression: "All thoughts of suicide, be gone." Say to the person in a coma: "Wake up." Do all of this IN THE NAME OF JESUS!

5. Try speaking to the injury or illness: "Pain, be gone in the name of Jesus." "Cancer, get out of this body." "Eating disorder, you have no place in the life of my friend _____."

6. Quote or read the verses as declarations of the promises of God you read in step two.

7. Find out if there has been any change in the person(s) for whom you have exercised this kind of declarative prayer. Thank God for using you if there has been breakthrough.

If you want to grow in the authority Jesus has given you, I would encourage you to practice this exercise at least ten times before you discount it as being too weird or too charismatic. I also recommend reading: *I Give You Authority: Practicing the Authority Jesus Gave Us* by Charles H. Kraft.

On a Personal Note

I have been turned off by healing evangelists who abuse their spiritual authority through the dramatic flair of sensationalism that seems to be more about them than about God's glory. Even so, I'm not going to let the abuses of some keep me from growing in exercising the authority I have to minister to people in God's power. I have a sense that I will have more and more stories to tell of dramatic, immediate results in healing as I keep applying what I'm learning here.

85

A PRAYER FOR HEALING

... pray for each other that you might be healed
(James 5:14).

Many Christians from Western cultures find it weird or (at least uncommon) to pray for sick people. For some, prayer is what you do if the doctors or medicine can't cure it, sort of the "last line of defense" when all else fails. For others, prayer for healing is relegated to the priest, pastor, or elder. It is disappointingly uncommon for Christ-followers to practice laying hands on sick people, praying for them to be healed, and expect that God will do something to make them better.

The following exercise is for any sincere believer to be obedient to the admonition we read in James and grow in the authority to heal that Jesus has entrusted to all of His followers (Mark 16:19).

1. When someone you know or meet is suffering from an illness, offer to pray for them (this first step often requires the most faith).

2. Explain to them why you want to pray. Here are some that I use depending on the situation:

    *   God has so graciously healed me so many times that I want to pass on this precious gift to others.

    *   Jesus did powerful healing miracles when He walked on this earth. After He was crucified God raised Him

from the dead and as He returned to heaven He sent His Holy Spirit to those of us who follow Him. That Spirit gives us power to heal sick people.

- The Bible teaches that I'm supposed to pray for the sick.

- Share a story of Jesus healing someone in the gospels or a contemporary testimony of Jesus healing someone through a prayer of faith.

3. Ask permission to pray for them on the spot, out loud (assure them that you won't cause a scene).

4. Ask them if you can place a hand on them.

5. Pray a simple prayer for healing. "Father, please heal _____ of his/her _____. We're not so sure we have enough faith for this. But we'll let you be the judge. I know you have great compassion for _____. Like a good father, You have compassion on Your son/daughter in this condition. So please demonstrate your love for _____ by showing your power to heal. We ask this in the name of Jesus."

6. Now ask: "Did you feel anything as we prayed?"

7. If there was any level of healing, relief or comfort, rejoice with the person who prayed for. If not, pray again. Commit to them to keep asking God for healing until there is relief.

On a Personal Note

I definitely don't have the gift of healing. But this doesn't stop me from believing that sometimes people will be dramatically healed or at least experience the presence of the Spirit through my prayers. This is a guess, but I suppose that at least three out of four of the people I pray for experience no immediate physical improvement at the moment I pray. I usually ask if there has been a change. But a number of people experience some sense of peace, comfort, or some other spiritual manifestation. Some feel more loved by God through these healing prayers. It seems that healing prayer often accelerates the healing process. And there are some cases where people were dramatically healed sometime after prayer, as in, waking up the next morning completely well. I am inspired to keep asking because I know Jesus always honors our obedience and acts of compassion. He is the healer. I just position myself for Him to work through me when I pray this way.

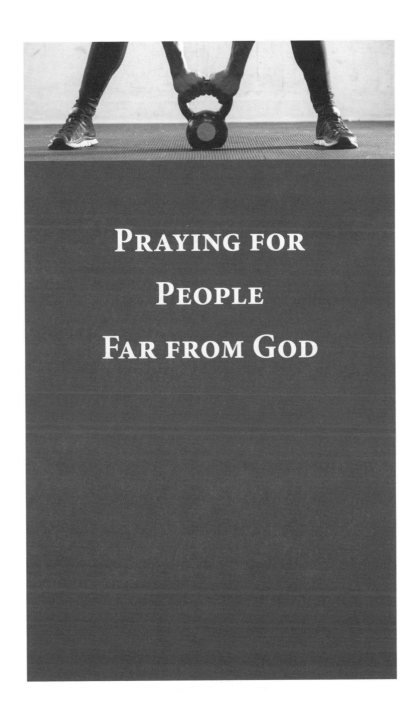

PRAYING FOR
PEOPLE
FAR FROM GOD

86

A HEART OF COMPASSION

But when He saw the multitudes,
He was moved with compassion for them, because they were
weary and scattered, like sheep having no shepherd
(Matthew 9:36 NKJV).

Jesus was often *moved with compassion* for people in need. Sometimes individuals, sometimes crowds. Sometimes he was stirred because of their spiritual need, as in the case above. Often, it was because of a physical or practical need. The phrase *moved with compassion*, or *had compassion* is from an interesting word in the original language of the New Testament. Its root is the word *splagne* which means "intestines!" One's gut was the seat of the emotions for Greek-speakers in the 1st Century. For us, our hearts are where we experience emotions.[27]

The bottom line is that Jesus cared deeply about the needs of others. When Jesus had compassion it was a deep emotional stirring, a longing that expressed the very heart of God. It is interesting that the grammatical structure of the verb moved with compassion is passive. In other words, Jesus didn't conjure it up or make himself feel compassion. It came upon him. I don't think it's a stretch to see this as the Spirit of God inciting in Jesus a divine, agape love. The same Spirit that stirred Jesus' heart with compassion can work in our hearts as well.

Here's a way in which we can have our hearts moved with His compassion.

1. Look up the word "compassion" or the phrase "moved with compassion" in the four gospels. There are some powerful Bible programs on line that make using a concordance seem obsolete. My favorite is BibleGateway.com.

2. What was the need that caused Jesus to be moved with compassion in each of these stories? How did He respond?

3. Ask the Holy Spirit to give us that compassion for people we know who are suffering in the ways that stirred Jesus. Ask Him to show you how to respond.

4. Go to a public place like a shopping mall. Find a place where you can watch the crowds pass. Rather than simply observing people, ask for the Father's heart for this crowd. Choose to *not* judge them or assume anything about the individuals that pass other than the fact that they are created in the image of God and that *He* ascribes immeasurable worth to each of them. He loves them so much He sent Jesus to die for them. Ask for God's supernatural love to move you to care that many of them are harassed and helpless, like sheep without a shepherd. [28]

5. When you are alone, place your hand over your heart (or if you speak Greek, your *splagne*) and pray: "Father, please fill my heart with Your divine compassion. Help me choose to love with Your unconditional, agape love." Pray this longing in your own words over and over until you sense it truly is the cry of your heart. Now place your hands over your eyes and pray: "Father, please help me see people through your eyes, eyes that look past outward appearances but instead to see with eyes that see Your image in people. To hold them in highest regard and immeasurable worth." Pray this in your own words repeating this desire until you sense a breakthrough.

How did that feel? If you didn't feel any immediate effects, don't worry. If you are like me you will be caught fighting back tears over the needs of others in times when you least expect it. God does hear our prayers!

On a Personal Note

I'm not a naturally compassionate person. The gift of mercy never shows up on my spiritual gifts assessment tests. However, I pray for compassion often. And by His grace I occasionally experience, in much smaller doses, what Jesus must have felt when he was moved with compassion.

One such occasion was when we were in the province of Ache in northwest Sumatera right after the devastating tsunami that resulted in nearly 200,000 casualties. We were there as translators with a medical team from our church. Helicopters dropped us into an area west of the coastal town of Tenom that had become a wasteland of mud and concrete foundations. We set up a temporary clinic in a mosque three kilometers inland and served over 300 people who had survived. Anyone who saw what we saw would have plenty of opportunity for compassion. Our team, however was almost too busy serving to be able to shed tears throughout that week. But on our last day there, the Spirit, who pours out God's love in our hearts (Romans 5:5) swept over me like a holy tsunami.

We were giving away the last of our medical supplies, our remaining food, our clothing except what we needed to wear home, and the remaining Rupiah we had in our possession when I lost it. I sobbed as I witnessed these Acehnese Muslims who had lost everything gratefully accepting our smelly clothes, our pocket change, and MREs (Meals Ready to Eat) that we would not be needing. That experience was so impactful that for months after returning home I would be stirred to tears remembering the faces and the pain of the people we had served.

87

Praying Jesus' Final Command

Then Jesus came to them and said, "All authority in heaven and on earth has been given to me. Therefore go and make disciples of all nations, baptizing them in the name of the Father and of the Son and of the Holy Spirit, and teaching them to obey everything I have commanded you. And surely I am with you always, to the very end of the age"
(Matthew 28:18-20).

This is such a familiar passage for many of us. Have you ever prayed it? I mean prayed it for yourself, as if this was Jesus last spoken command directed to you?

1. Read the three verses above out loud.

2. Look for the four verbs in verses 19-20. One is the main verb and the other three are participles. What you find is: (While) *going, make disciples, baptizing,* and *teaching* (training)....

3. Now imagine yourself as part of the group Jesus gathered around Him as He is about to ascend to heaven after His forty days of hanging out with His followers and teaching them about the Kingdom. Hear Him give this command to you personally.

4. Now ask: "Lord, show me, speak to me. How am I doing at making disciples? How about going? Baptizing, and training these disciples to obey?"

5. Write down what you are hearing. Be honest. He will not condemn you but you may have a new awareness of how profoundly clear these four activities should be part of our lifestyle.

6. Ask, "Lord, who are you calling me to make your disciple?"

7. Please show me how and where you would want me:
   - to go
   - to baptize
   - to train disciples to obey your commands

8. Write down what you are hearing. Following through with obedience usually means starting to share the gospel with the persons you know who are not yet Jesus followers.

9. If there is loving accountability in your Christian community, you will be more likely to be bold and caring enough to overcome fear and timidity.

On a Personal Note

This is one of the most challenging exercises of all the 101 you find in this book. Not the prayer part, but the follow-through. May God give you grace to embrace a lifestyle of making disciples!

88

YOUR MOST WANTED LIST

All of us know people who have yet to experience the transforming love of Jesus Christ. They have yet to admit their need for a Savior, to turn from their sins and trust in what Jesus death purchased for them—complete and total forgiveness of every selfish choice, every vile and shameful thing they've ever done. They have yet to give themselves to God. They have yet to experience what is very familiar to us: a squeaky clean conscience and a heart overflowing with the reality that we are loved by God! They have never felt the sweet presence of the Spirit of God (I could go on and on.) Maybe they've heard and responded with a "No" or "Not yet." Maybe they've never really heard.

Either way, here's a powerful tool to keep us crying out to God on their behalf.

1. Make a list of at least five people you know who fit the above category. Keep your list to ten or less. Ask God who should be on your first list. It's more effective if these are people you are interacting with on a regular basis.

2. Call out their names to God and pray the following verses for them:

- 1 Thessalonians 1:5-7,9
- 2 Corinthians 4:3-4
- Romans 10:9-10,13-14
- Acts 2:37-38; 3:19-20; 4:12,30; 16:14; 17:30; 26:18
- John 1:12; 3:16; 6:44; 7:37-38; 14:6; 16:8
- Revelation 3:20
- Pray any other promise from God's Word that comes to mind.

3. As you pray imagine yourself sharing the love of Christ with them and admonishing them: "Be reconciled to God" (2 Corinthians 5:20).

4. Keep your list handy. Pray for them often.

5. One way to remember them and to pray consistently for them with passion is to create a photo album with their pictures. Let their faces scroll on your screen saver.

6. What fun it will be as people on your most wanted list are scratched off as they follow Christ!

On a Personal Note

When creating a photo album with my most wanted list, I obviously needed photos! For some, I did not already have a picture. So I shamelessly asked to take their pictures so I could remember to pray for them to turn to Christ.

89

PRAYER TRIPLETS

*Again, truly I tell you that if two of you on earth
agree about anything they ask for, it will be done for
them by my Father in heaven*
(Matthew 18:19).

This exercise is similar to the previous one, but as "Prayer
Triplets" implies, you are joining two others as the three
of you pray for three people (nine total) who are far from
Christ. Our prayers are exponentially effective when prayed
in agreement with other faith-filled believers.

Here's how it works:

1. In a group of three, give opportunity for each person to
   share the names of three people they are believing God
   for to come to saving faith. Group members share about
   their connection to each person and what is known about
   their spiritual condition and underlying beliefs.

2. Now that nine names are on the table, pray prayers from
   the following passages:
   - 1 Thessalonians 1:5-7, 9
   - 2 Corinthians 4:3-4
   - Romans 10:9-10, 13-14
   - Acts 2:37-38; 3:19-20; 4:12,30; 16:14; 17:30; 26:18
   - John 1:12; 3:16; 6:44; 7:37-38; 14:6; 16:8
   - Revelation 3:20
   - Add other prayers as you are lead

3. Commit to pray for all nine on a regular basis. Let the group determine how often you will pray.

4. Report progress and spiritual breakthroughs with each other. See your faith grow and people come into the Kingdom.

On a Personal Note

Janine and I recently shared this prayer exercise with a group of Indonesian Christians. They formed groups of three and proceeded to pray for their friends and family member far from Christ. That was a Friday. By that Sunday, within forty-eight hours, some of the people they had just begun to pray for communicated a new spiritual hunger, on their own initiative! Coincidence? I don't think so.

90

Praying for
Missionaries

*And pray for me, too. Ask God to give me the right words
so I can boldly explain God's mysterious plan that the
Good News is for Jews and Gentiles alike*
(Ephesians 6:19).

You may know some missionaries personally. Are you ever at a loss as to how to pray for them?

The following exercise will help you broaden the ways to pray based on God's Word:

1. Take a few minutes and express gratitude to God for the missionaries you are about to pray for. Thank God for their commitment, sacrifice, and specific things you know about them.

2. If you have a recent prayer update from them pray for specific, personal needs that they have communicated.

3. Now read from the following Bible passages and turn what you read into a prayer. I will give you a couple of examples. Put these prayers into your own words:

   - Ephesians 6:19: "Lord, please give _____ the right words, the ability to communicate the Gospel clearly and in such a way their target people understand it." Give them boldness.

- Colossians 4:3: "Please give our friends _____ open doors and opportunities to share with people who have never heard."

- Luke 10:6; Matthew 4:20: "Please lead _____ to 'People of Peace' who will receive them and their message. Let the people they encounter be like soil of the fourth type—people who will in turn be faithful and fruitful to lead many others to Jesus."

- 1 Corinthians 2:4: "May _____ not only communicate clearly the message of your kingdom, but be used by You to do the works of Your Kingdom." "Demonstrate your power as they share with and pray for people." "Give them faith to lay hands on sick people and see them recover."

- John 15:5-8: "May they enjoy sweet intimacy with you, consistently." May they see much fruit from their lives and labor there in _____ and may this bring great glory to you, Father."

- 2 Corinthians 4:15: "Father, please make _____ really effective as your grace flows through him/her/them to reach more and more people so that there will be more thanksgiving for you and so that you will receive more and more glory."

4. Take note of special or specific ways in which the Holy Spirit is leading you to pray. He will probably lead you to other portions of Scripture to pray apart from those identified here. He may even give you promises or a prophetic picture for you to pray.

5. Take a few minutes and email these impressions, promises, and words of encouragement to the missionary you've been praying for. This will be a great encouragement.

On a Personal Note

We have been on both the praying end and receiving end of prayers for missionaries for decades now. Any and all fruitfulness we have experienced has been the direct result of people praying for us. Words can't express the gratitude we feel for people who pray for us. The emails we receive from the gracious, faithful prayer warriors, sharing impressions they receive as they pray, are like icing on the cake. So precious.

91

10/40 WINDOW PRAYER

The harvest is great, but the workers are few.
So pray to the Lord who is charge of the harvest: Ask Him to
send more workers into the fields
(Matthew 9:37-38).

The 10/40 window is that part of our world where the least number of people know about Jesus and have little or no access to His message. It roughly corresponds with the swath of the globe between ten and forty degrees north of the equator starting with the western coast of north Africa stretching eastward through Indonesia. Many of us pray for this region of the world but the following exercise can help us be more consistent in praying for the people on our planet who have the least opportunity of encountering a Christian, a Bible, a church, or the life-changing message of the cross.

Here's a simple way to remember:

1. Set your watch alarm to go off at 10:40 a.m. and/or 10:40 p.m.

2. When the alarm goes off, take at least five minutes and cry out to God for the people of this part of our planet.

3. Pray for missionaries you know working in that part of the world. Use exercise ninety-three if you need help in knowing specifically what to pray.

4. If God has put a specific country or better yet a specific people group on your heart, see what Joshua Project (www.JoshuaProject.net) has to say about the spiritual condition of that nation or people group.

5. Pray:

   - For workers to be sent to the harvest (Matthew 9:37-38). Ask God for more faith-filled, bold, faithful seed-sowers of the Gospel.

   - For their effective, cross-cultural communication. Unreached peoples need Jesus' disciples from other cultures to cross language and culture barriers.

   - For the power of God to be demonstrated as the Gospel is preached (Acts 11:21).

   - That the word of God would spread rapidly and for there to be many new believers (Acts 12:24).

   - If you have done exercise eighty-three, pray some of your best prayers from other verses in Acts.

6. Pray for groups of new disciples to form. Pray that these budding groups would transform into fully functioning churches that will multiply rapidly.

7. Pray that as they experience persecution (and they will), they will not shrink back but would be bold even if they face suffering and death. Pray that they may experience the same passion that they early believers experienced when they were persecuted: "'And now, O Lord, hear their threats, and give us, your servants, great boldness in preaching your word. Stretch out your hand with healing power; may miraculous signs and wonders be done through the name of your holy servant Jesus.' After this prayer, the meeting place shook, and they were all filled with the Holy Spirit. Then they preached the word of God with boldness" (Acts 4:29-31 NLT).

8. Close out your prayer with thanksgiving to God for hearing these requests.

On a Personal Note

Be careful if you pray this exercise often. You may make a life-altering decision like leaving the comfort, security, and familiarity of your home culture and moving to somewhere in the 10/40 window as part of God's way of answering your prayers!

92

PRAYING FOR MUSLIMS

There are currently 2.08 billion Muslims on our planet. Very few of them know who Jesus (Isa) is and what He did for them through His sacrificial death on the cross. Very few of them have a personal relationship with a sincere Jesus follower. Even fewer have someone praying for them by name. Wouldn't the Father be pleased with people who care enough to pray for Muslims in general and specific Muslims we may know?

Here are some specific ways to pray for Muslims:

1. Spend a few minutes thanking God for a Muslim you may know who has put their faith in Jesus and/or a breakthrough among Muslims you may have heard of where many have come to Christ.

2. Now, bring before the Father the names of Muslims you may know personally, people groups you may have heard of, or Muslim nations of our world.[29]

3. Pray the following passages with faith and fervor.
   - 1 Thessalonians 1:5-7, 9
   - 2 Corinthians 4:3-4
   - Romans 10:9-10, 13-14
   - Acts 2:37-38; 3:19-20; 4:12,30; 16:14; 17:30; 26:18
   - John 1:12; 3:16; 6:44; 7:37-38; 14:6; 16:8
   - Revelation 3:20

4. Here are other Muslim-specific prayers you can pray:

- Ask God to make them deeply dissatisfied with their religious striving to be good enough.

- Invite the Holy Spirit to show them that all their efforts cannot earn forgiveness or a right-standing with their Creator.

- Pray for many more Muslims to have dreams and visions of Isa. Muslims are having dreams of a man with a kind, radiant face (often wearing a white robe) saying: "I am the way, the truth, and the life. Come and follow me."

- Pray for Muslims to witness dramatic answers to prayer prayed by authentic Jesus followers that result in healing, deliverance, and other miracles. May their response be like that of those in Samaria in Acts 8:6-12.

- Pray that compassionate, bold Jesus followers will share the gospel in culturally relevant ways with clarity and power. Ask for liberal sowing of acts of mercy and compassion along with liberal sowing of the Good News.

- Pray for rapidly reproducing groups of new disciples who are obedient to Jesus' commands, especially the last one: the Great Commission (Matthew 28:18-20).

- Pray that new disciples will remain faithful and bold despite suffering and persecution.

On a Personal Note

I recently traveled to an area where the population is 99.9% Muslim with the express purpose of engaging as many as possible in spiritual conversations and to pray directly for people to experience God's empowering presence. The Lord opened the door for the mayor of one of the towns in the area to hear the Good News. He seemed rather unresponsive until I offered to pray for any ailments he was suffering. He welcomed prayer, even prayer in Jesus' name. I prayed a simple prayer for the pain in both of his legs to go away. I then asked how it felt as we prayed. He said: "O, the pain is still there, but when you prayed I felt waves of peace wash over the stress I've been experiencing." I love it. I'm convinced that the grace I have to reach out and love Muslims in Jesus' name is directly related to praying for them.

93

Praying for Hindus

*We have come to bring you the Good News that you should
turn from these worthless things and turn to the living God,
who made heaven and earth, the sea, and everything in them*
(Acts 14:15).

There are at least 1.08 billion Hindus in our world today.
At least 996,000 live in India. Most of these nearly one
billion Indian Hindus believe that their sins can be washed
away if they dip themselves into the Mother Ganges River. They
believe that there are countless gods and goddesses, ancestor
spirits and other spirits living in trees, animals, and certain
geographic locations. These gods are worshipped by Hindus
all over the world. New Age is a form of Hinduism growing
in popularity in the West. But there are significant numbers of
new Jesus followers among Hindus in India. Prayer has been
a huge factor in these movements in which over a million
Hindus have "turned from idols to serve the true and living
God" (1 Thessalonians 1:9).

Here are some ways we can pray.

1. Spend a few minutes thanking God for a Hindu you may
    know who has put their faith in Jesus and/or a break-
    through among Hindus you may have heard of where
    many have come to Christ.

2. Now, bring before the Father the names of Hindus you may know personally, people groups you may have heard of, or Hindu nations of our world.[30]

3. Pray the following passages with faith and fervor.

   - 1 Thessalonians 1:5-7, 9
   - 2 Corinthians 4:3-4
   - Romans 10:9-10, 13-14
   - Acts 2:37-38; 3:19-20; 4:12,30; 16:14; 17:30; 26:18
   - John 1:12; 3:16; 6:44; 7:37-38; 14:6; 16:8
   - Revelation 3:20

4. Here are some Hindu-specific prayers:

   "Lord Jesus …

   - "May all Hindus, including the New Age converts in Western nations, become deeply disillusioned with their gods 'who are mere idols' (Psalm 96:5). Expose the spirits of darkness behind these deities.

   - "Send compassionate, bold, Spirit-filled Jesus-followers who will clearly communicate the Good News to Hindus in culturally relevant ways.

   - "Demonstrate that Jesus Christ is above every name that can be invoked, high above the millions of Hindu gods (see Ephesians 1:21) through miraculous answers to prayer on the part of Christians. Work powerfully through healing people and delivering them from evil spirits. We ask for power encounters.

   - "Draw a stark contrast in the minds of Hindus between the grace, beauty, majesty, and love of our Living God and the character of the petty, wicked deities they attempt to appease out of fear.

   - "For those who hear about Jesus or watch the Jesus Film, may they understand the exclusive claims of

Jesus and worship Him alone—renouncing all other gods and goddesses.

- "May the disciple-making movements among people groups in India spread to other castes both in India and other nations.

- "May Hindu background believers and all those reaching out to Hindus stand firm when they face pushback and persecution from the Hindu authorities. May they be like the early disciples who 'rejoice that they would be counted worthy to suffer for the name of Jesus' (see Acts 5:41). May they faithfully continue to sow the Good News." [31]

On a Personal Note

I was recently reminded of the importance of the power dynamic in the Hindu worldview. A church-planter I coach here on Bali was asked by the manager of a hotel if he could pray for one of his staff who was being harassed by evil spirits. "Sure," my friend said. It took three prayer sessions to help this beautiful young Balinese Hindu gal get delivered from the demons who were ravaging her. She experienced a dramatic transformation through a radical conversion to Christ. Since then she has, in turn, shared her Jesus encounter with her friends and family. She has even gone to hospitals and prayed for healing and freedom for other Hindus. At least six other Hindus are now following Jesus as a result of this power encounter.

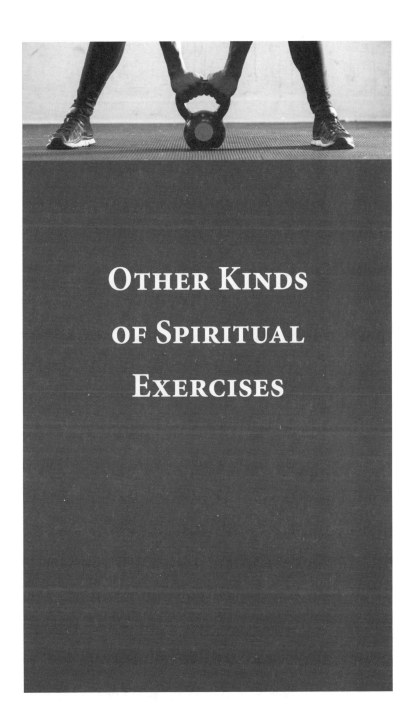

OTHER KINDS
OF SPIRITUAL
EXERCISES

94

Praying Biographies: Bible Heroes

And now, brothers and sisters, we want you to know about the grace that God has given the Macedonian churches (2 Corinthians 8:1).

When the Apostle Paul wanted to inspire the Corinthian believers to give generously, he used the example of the Macedonians. Hearing of other's sacrifice, faith, courage, or character tends to inspire us to new levels of commitment. This exercise can help us take note of the faith of others and pray specifically for things in their lives that pleased God.

It goes like this:

1. Select one of your favorite heroes of the faith in the Bible.

2. Look up every Bible reference you can find about them.

3. What about them do you admire? Make a list.

4. From what you know about God, what do you think God loved about this person? Add to your list anything else that comes to mind.

5. Thank God for what you observe in him/her.

6. Now from this list ask God to form in you these same character traits.

On a Personal Note

One of my many heroes in the Bible is Epaphras. He shows up in only three short verses (Colossians 1:7; 4:12; Philemon 23), but I love what is said about him. We surmise that he was one of those who came to faith in Ephesus during Paul's time there. He was probably trained at the *Tyrannus discipleship school*.[32] He then returned home to Colosse and communicated the gospel to the people and undoubtedly had a significant role in starting the church there. That's impressive enough according to me. Add to this three other things Paul says about him: 1) He is a *dulos*, a "slave" of Christ; 2) He always wrestles in prayer for his fellow-believers in Colosse; 3) He ended up in jail for his faith (Philemon 23).

Here's part of my prayer inspired by Epaphras: "Father, thank you for Epaphras. I love the fact that he cared enough about the people of his hometown that he made sure they heard about Jesus and a church came out of His witness there. I so want to be as faithful a witness as he was." Even more challenging for me is the fact that he *always wrestled in prayer* for them once the church was established and he was no longer there. So my prayer continues: "Help me, Father, to stand up for for the people I've seen come to faith—the people of the churches that I helped start. Please help me emulate Epaphras' servant heart and embolden me to be willing to suffer for my faith. Amen"

95

Praying Biographies: Church History Heroes

Remember your leaders, who spoke the word of God to you.
Consider the outcome of their way of life
and imitate their faith
(Hebrews 13:7).

This exercise is similar to the previous one. The people we choose to imitate here are not found in the Bible but have had great impact in our world. It may be a person who led you to Christ or who has mentored you on your journey. He or she may have left a profound impression on you. You could also choose a well-known Christian leader from present or past who you don't know personally. I am a student of church history so there are hundreds of persons I have read about who, when I consider the outcome of their way of life, find much to consider and pray about.

Here is how to go about it.

1. Pick one of your favorite heroes of the faith from the options listed above.

2. What about them do you admire?[33]

3. From what you know about God, what do you think God loved about this person?

4. Thank God for what you observe in him/her.

5. Now from this list ask God to form in you these same character traits.

On a Personal Note

Ever since I read about Raymond Lull (1232-1315) I have had a godly envy of the impact of his life. He lived during the Crusades, an age in which most leaders in Christendom (with the notable exception of Francis of Assisi) considered that "the only good Muslim is a dead Muslim." No one considered sharing the gospel with Muslims in hopes that one would follow Jesus. That is, no one except Raymond Lull.

He dared to care and became a pioneer in missions. His conversion alone is a fascinating read. He was a philosopher, theologian, artist, scholar, a mathematician, and a mechanical engineer. But most impressive to me is that he had a life-long passion to share the gospel with the Muslim world. He learned Arabic. He interacted with Muslim scholars and crafted a system of apologetics in an attempt to convince Muslims of the merits of Christianity.

He traveled throughout Europe meeting with church leaders including the Pope, trying to convince them to establish training institutions to mobilize well-prepared missionaries for the Muslim world. He was about seven centuries ahead of his time! He lived and died for what he believed. He led at least four missionary journeys to North Africa to preach the Gospel. On his last journey he was beaten to death while preaching in what is now Algeria. Talk about prayer fodder!

96

CRAFTED PRAYERS

This exercise is designed to help you create prayers that you will want to re-pray over and over. These crafted prayers don't come from a prayer book as someone else's prayers, but rather are birthed from the sincere longings of your own heart. They are personal. You may not be a poet and the prayers you craft may seem clunky and chaotic, but if they represent the longings of the depth of your soul, they can become significant weapons in your prayer arsenal. "There can be a power, beauty, and precision of thought expressed in our crafted prayers. It's like writing poetry to your sweetheart as opposed to depending on your extemporaneous expression of a stream of consciousness (to carry the analogy further, a poem that you write, however clumsy and awkward, would probably have a greater impact on him/her than something composed by Shakespeare or a Hallmark card writer."[34]

The beauty of a crafted prayer is that it's a tool you can pull out of your toolkit and repeat as often as you would like, but you are not slavishly bound to pray it the same way every time. There is freedom to expound on what you've written. It's like giving a speech from a prepared outline. Sometimes, the most profound thing you might say is when you veer off from your notes. But it's still good to have notes.

Here is the process:

1. Pick a topic you find yourself praying about a lot. Here are some examples: Love, Joy, Boldness, Success in My Work, Prayers for My Wife, Prayers for My kids, Peace, A Heart for Lost People, Living in the Authority Jesus Gave Me, Finances, The Things I Want Most in Life, et cetera

2. Using a Bible program or concordance, compile a list of the verses in the Bible on your topic.

3. Read the verses and meditate on them.

4. Create a first draft and began to "pray it on for size."

5. Revise it and reword it as many times as you need to. I have updated my prayer for Growing in Love at least twenty times.

6. You may go through seasons when you pray a particular crafted prayer often. Others may seem less pressing. No worries. Just follow the Spirit's leading and the longings of your heart.

On a Personal Note

I keep my crafted prayers on my tablet. Rarely does a day go by that I don't pray at least one of them. I also create new ones every couple of months. To see some examples of my crafted prayers see Appendix C.

97

A Crafted Prayer for My Spouse

Spiritual intimacy in relationships is enhanced through consistently praying together and also by praying for each other. This reality is most evident in a marriage relationship. Of all the people in the world I am called to love, my spouse is my first priority, and what better way can I love someone than by praying? The problem is when I remember to pray for her, I can't remember what would be most important to pray.

This simple exercise will you know how you can best love your spouse through some specific prayers.

1. Make a list of five things you love most about your husband or wife. Now you have created the best way to begin to pray for him/her: gratitude expressed to God. Pray what you've written.

2. What are the things your spouse wants most in life at this time? Write down what comes to mind.

3. Having started your crafted prayer for your spouse, it's time to ask her/him directly: "How can I pray for you?" "I am making a commitment to God to pray for you more consistently and I would like to hear from you what you really want most in life at this time." If they've created their own prayer for what they really want most in life (see

Exercise 54), ask if it would be okay to incorporate those things in your prayer for them.

4. Can you think of any promises in the Bible that relate to their desires? Incorporate them in your crafted prayer.

5. Once you've completed your first draft pray it out loud for them in their presence.

6. Invite their input.

7. Commit to God and your spouse regarding how often or how long you intend to pray this prayer. For example, you may have the grace to commit to twenty-one straight days of praying this prayer.

8. When you begin to see breakthrough, celebrate together.

9. Periodically, revise and update your prayer. We are growing and dynamically changing from season to season, and prayers need to change too.

On a Personal Note

As with any crafted prayer, feel free to vary the way you pray these things. Remember these written prayers are like notes for a speech. A speech that's rehearsed without engaging fresh thoughts and emotions can be really lifeless. You have the freedom to be spontaneous.

98

Highs and Lows of My Day

Rejoice with those who rejoice, and weep
with those who weep
(Romans 12:15).

This simple exercise works well for family devotions at the end of the day or as a way to get people praying for each other in a small group community.

Here's how it goes.

1. Read or quote Romans 12:15. We want to share what brought us joy today and what made us sad or was hard for us today (or this week). Let's start with our highs; the joys that we can celebrate.

2. Now what has been a low point (difficult, sad, challenging)?

3. Take time to rejoice with each other in prayer and to bear each other's burdens.

On a Personal Note

Our family often interacted around the dinner table with this simple exercise. It was not always serious. Funny and even embarrassing stories were common. All of us are convinced that this simple, focused conversation contributed to our family's continued emotional closeness even now when everyone is an adult and we all live in different cities.

99

WHO GOD SAYS I AM

For we are God's handiwork... (work of art, masterpiece)
(Ephesians 2:10a).

A m I the only one, or do you also feel insecure at times? Even we who have a strong self-image find ourselves filled with self-doubt and insecurity on occasion. We have several options in our insecurity: 1) We can try to obtain a sense of security through what we obtain or accomplish; 2) We can compare ourselves with people we consider inferior to us in order to feel a sense of worth; 3) We can determine our identity by what God says about us. The Bible is full of affirmation about us as God's children, starting with Genesis 1:26 when God decided to make us "in His image."

Emotionally healthy Christ-followers know that no matter what we feel in the moment, we are loved by God. Just saying that brings security. Imagine what it would be like if you often thought about and thanked God for what He says about you!

Here's an exercise that puts to flight our insecurities.

1. Make a list of statements from what we know from the Bible about who God says we are. At the top of the list write: By God's grace and the work of Christ through His suffering death and resurrection I am .... Here are a few examples from my list (for my complete list see Appendix D).

I am:

- God's possession—I belong to Him (2 Corinthians 5:14-15; 1 Peter 2:9; 1 Timothy 6:11).
- Near to God, by the blood of Jesus Christ (Ephesians 2:13).
- Made holy in Jesus Christ (1 Corinthians 1:2).
- Able to do all things through Him who gives me strength (Philippians 4:13).

2. Now declare them. If you are alone, try shouting them out.

3. Add to this list through your personal Bible reading. You will be amazed at how much the Bible says about our identity in Christ. Ephesians 1-3, Colossians 1-2, and Romans 1-8 are particularly rich in these foundational truths about who we are because of Christ.

4. Pull out this list and read it as prayers next time you are hammered by insecurity, self-doubt, or condemnation.

On a Personal Note

Sometimes I experience prayer like water-skiing. There's a fair amount of drag as the boat is working to get you out of and on top of the water. When I was first learning to ski, I just let go of the rope when it got too hard. But once you learn the joy of sliding across the top of the water you endure the initial strain. Often this prayer exercise pulls me out of the negative emotions, feelings of defeat or condemnation, or even just the hassles of life. I begin to feel on top of the water or to be more biblical, I feel *raised up with Christ and seated with Him in the heavenly realm*[35] when I pray this way.[35]

100

Destiny Revelation Experiences

Most of us have experienced special moments in our lives when we realize the God has a unique purpose for us. God reveals His purpose, His destiny for us, in a variety of ways.

This exercise will help us reflect on some of these experiences. Let me warn you: you will be humbled by the reality of God's mighty hand on your life.

1. Center your heart on God in a place that's quiet when you have at least an hour to reflect and pray (this one can't be done "on the run").

2. Pray: "Holy Spirit anoint my memory. Please bring to mind things about my destiny in you that I need to remember." Now, think through your life with the following questions:

    - Were there special circumstances surrounding your birth? Perhaps your parents were childless for years because they couldn't conceive and then you came along? Maybe your mother wanted to abort you or you survived a medical crisis in which the odds of your survival were nil. These are clear signs of you having a special destiny in God! Maybe you were adopted. God had some special plans for you through the influence of your adopted parents.

- Consider your heritage. Perhaps the family you were born into had a rich spiritual legacy. The spiritual footprints they have left behind are indications that God was working long before you were born. Maybe the opposite is true. Perhaps you are a "trophy of grace," you were redeemed out of a family of criminals, idol worshippers, or cult members. God is to be praised either way.

- Where or how you were raised? For example, I spent the ages of ten to seventeen in the Rio Grande Valley of Texas. Relating to people with a language and culture different than mine was a critical piece in God preparing me for my life calling.

- What about your name? Maybe the meaning of your name has significance for God's calling on your life.

- Think about prophetic words you have received. Sometimes prophetic words spoken over children carry huge weight in a person's calling in God. Even as adults, God can speak to us through these kinds of words.

- What about dreams? Has God given you or someone else a special dream that points to God's plan for your life?

- What were the events surrounding your conversion? God has initiated relationship with each of us who know His love. To some degree our faith story speaks to us of His purpose for our lives. What about yours?

- Think of other experiences that you have had that speak to God mighty hand on your life. Perhaps you've had supernatural leading or encounters in the choices you've made. Pause and ask Him again to show you anything else.

3. Take time to thank God and praise Him for the ways He has shown you that you have a purpose in Him. Express a humility that the God who created the universe would choose you to be part of His great plan.

4. Ask Him if there are other things He would want to reveal to you about His purpose for you.

5. Finally, ask: "Father, are there specific ways You want me to adjust my life in order to fulfill this great plan You had when You created me and called me to Yourself?

6. Write out all of this in your prayer journal.

On a Personal Note

I am greatly indebted to the teaching and writing of J. Robert (Bobby) Clinton for this exercise.[36] I first took time to reflect on the dozen or so destiny revelation experiences in my life when Dr. Clinton introduced me to this idea over twenty years ago. It had a profound impact on my sense of calling. It caused me to be more focused and more purposeful. Several of my key life decisions since that time have been influenced by this exercise.

101

DISCERNING GOD'S PURPOSE FOR MY LIFE

God has made us what we are. God has created us in King Jesus for the good works that He prepared, ahead of time, as the road we must travel" (Ephesians 2:10 TKNT).

As Christians we know God has called us to Himself to let His life flow through us to others. Jesus called it *bearing fruit*. Paul describes it as the *good works* that God has prepared for us. He has given us unique talents and abilities. Even our personalities and life experiences contribute to His ultimate purpose for us. Beyond these natural attributes are spiritual gifts. These are special, even supernatural abilities to do things that we can do only through the power of the Holy Spirit. Every one of us who loves Jesus wants to know what this God-given purpose is.

I have found the following exercise to be helpful is discovering how God tends to use me and thus how *He wants to work through me in the future.*

1. Find a time and place where you can be alone for the next hour. Center your heart through prayers of gratitude, adoration, and submission.

2. When have you most felt God's pleasure in what you were doing? There's an unforgettable scene in the movie Chariots of Fire where Eric Liddell, the Scottish gold medalist in the 1920 Olympics says: "I believe that God made me for a purpose. But He also made me fast, and when I run, I feel His pleasure." [37] Think of specific experiences in your life when you felt God's pleasure in your work or activities to which you were devoting yourself. You might have thought: "I was made for this". Come up with at least five.

3. Relive these events. Remember how it felt on each occasion. Reflect on the impact of what you did. How were the people experiencing you effected? Was there lasting fruit? How did God show you He was pleased?

4. Consider the experiences more deeply. Is there a pattern? Is there a consistent way God has seemed to work through you? How might He be wanting to use you more in this way? What adjustments do you need to make in your life to see this happen?

5. Are there dreams regarding how God might want to use your life that are yet to be realized?

6. Journal your answers and other thoughts. Interact with God in all of this.

On a Personal Note

How fitting that this last exercise is the one that inspired the compilation, writing, and the publishing of these 101 prayer exercises. Twenty years ago when I asked myself the questions above, I reflected on how much I loved training young Indonesian church planters in how to make time for daily prayer that they actually enjoyed. I sensed God's pleasure in inspiring and instructing people in ways to connect with Him through the spiritual disciplines.

When I became a pastor in Texas, that pattern continued with young leaders in our church. At the age of forty I came to believe that one legacy that I wanted to leave at the end of the journey was a life of devotion that inspired others to delight in a sincere, life-giving, growing, joy-filled relationship with God. The writing of this prayer manual is just one expression of that passion and desire.

Endnotes

1. O'brien, SJ, *Father Kevin Exploring the Spiritual Exercises of St. Ignatius in Daily Life* 9% in Kindle Version

2. What would really be great is to have a number of people comment on each exercise and even rate them. Maybe in my next edition, or on a website.

3. Jim works at the Center for Relational Care. www.relationalcare.org/

4. Vosscamp, Ann *One Thousand Gifts: A Dare to Live Fully Right Where You Are*, Zondervan 2011

5. *The Book of Common Prayer* has been the standard prayer book of the Church of England since 1549. It contains some time tested and dynamic prayers.

6. Still available in Kindle Edition found under the title *Could You Not Tarry: Learning the Joy of Prayer* by Larry Lea

7. Swaymakers.org for obtaining current and past prayer guides.

8. Boyd, Greg, *Seeing is Believing: Experiencing Jesus Through Imaginative Prayer* Baker Books 2004

9. Wikipedia article on Count Ludwig Von Zinzendorf

10. www.goodreads.com/.../4645522.Charles_Grandison_Finny

11. Thibodeaux S.J., Mark E. *Armchair Mystic: Easing Into Contemplative Prayer*, Saint Anthony Messenger Press 2001

12. Scazzero, Peter *Emotionally Heathy Spirituality* Zondervan 2006, Chapter 8

13. See my book *From Duty to Delight: Finding Greater Joy in Daily Prayer,*

14. 1 Timothy 2:9

15. Daniel Chapter 9

16. ignitinghope.com/hope

17. ibid

18. There's some fascinating research about the medical and physical benefits of fasting. Joel Furhman has some convincing data in his book *Fasting and Eating for Health: A Medical Doctor's Program for Conquering Disease* St. Martin's Press 1995. More recent research has shown that even a twenty-four hour fast once or twice a week has significant impact on cognitive ability and the prevention of Alzheimer's Disease.

19. O'brien, SJ, Father Kevin E*xploring the Spiritual Exercises of St. Ignatius in Daily Life* 9% in Kindle Version 42% in Kindle version

20. These quotes come from Frank Laubach come from Greg *Boyd's Present Perfect,* Zondervan 2010

21. Ibid

22. Cole, Neil *Cultivating a Life for God,* ChurchSmart Resources and CMA Resources, 1999

23. http://www.fbcdurham.org/wp *An Approach to Extended Memorization of Scripture* by Dr Andrew Davis

24. Ibid, page 3

25. Lord of the Rings: The Fellowship of the Ring 2001 Movie

26. See *I Give You Authority: Practicing the Authority Jesus Gave Us* by Charles H. Kraft. I highly recommend this and any of his other books on this subject to learn more about living in His authority over the dark forces.

27. In the Indonesian language you feel things in your hati which is your kidneys!

28. Greg Boyd tells a great story of his experience at a mall where he asked God to help him have compassion for people. You can find it on his sermon podcasts from series at Woodland Hills Church 6/9/2013 called "The Cross and the Tree". His story inspired this exercise.

29. Joshua Project (www.joshuaproject.net) has some great people profiles of the Muslim people groups.

30. Joshua Project (www.joshuaproject.net) has some great people profiles of the Hindu people groups.

31. Some have asked why not a specific way of praying for Buddhist, Jews, or Animists? Three reasons: 1) Muslim and Hindu People Groups represent the vast majority of Non-Christians in our world today; 2) I don't have a lot of experience praying for groups other than Muslims and Hindus; 3) I felt I had given enough to spiritual exercises praying for people far from Christ.

32. See Acts 19:8-10

33. Wikipedia can be a helpful tool here.

34. Parrish, Ron *From Duty to Delight: Finding Greater Joy in Daily Prayer,* CrossWay Books 2010, pg. 89

35. Ephesians 2:5-6

36. Clinton, Dr. J. Robert *The Making of a Leader* Barnabas Press, 1994

37. www.imdb.com/title/tt0082158/quotes

Bibliography

Boyd, Greg *Seeing is Believing: Experiencing Jesus Through Imaginative Prayer,* Baker Books (2004)

Boyd, Greg *Present Perfect,* Zondervan (2010)

Cole, Neil *Cultivating a Life for God,* ChurchSmart Resources and CMA Resources, (1999)

Clinton, Dr. J. Robert *The Making of a Leader,* Barnabas Press (1994)

Foster, Richard J. *Devotional Classics: Selected Readings for Individuals and Groups,* Zondervan (2005)

Foster, Richard J., *The Celebration of Discipline,* Harper Collins (1978)

Kraft, Charles H. *I Give You Authority: Practicing the Authority Jesus Gave Us,* Chosen (2012)

Lee, Larry *Could You Not Tarry One Hour?,* Charisma House (1987)

Newell, Phillip *Celtic Prayers from Iona,* Paulist Press (1997)

O'brien, SJ, Father Kevin *Exploring the Spiritual Exercises of St. Ignatius in Daily Life,* Loyola Press (2001)

Parrish, Ron *From Duty to Delight: Finding Greater Joy in Daily Prayer,* CrossWay Books (2010)

Scazzero, Pete *Emotionally Heathy Spirituality,* Zondervan (2006)

Shawchuck, Norman and Ruben P. Job *Celtic Daily Prayer for ALL Who Seek God*, Upper Room Books 2013

Thibodeaux, Mark E., *Armchair Mystic: Easing Into Contemplative Prayer*, St. Anthony Messenger Press (1989)

Tickle, Phylilis *The Divine Hours*, Oxford University Press (2007)

Vosscamp, Ann (2011) *One Thousand Gifts: A Dare to Live Fully Right Where You Are*, Zondervan

Appendix A

ABCs of Adoration
An example of A,B and C

A wesome, attractive, able, abundant, absolute, Adonai, abiding, approachable, amazing, affirming, accepting, assessable, affectionate, all-knowing, almighty, always, appealing, attentive, awe-inspiring, anointed, alpha, active, alive, above all, all in all, Allah, and authentic.

B lessed, beautiful, bountiful, brilliant, beloved, believable, better, big, boundless, bidding, blameless, and benevolent

C aring, compassionate, capable, captivating, constant, colorful, communicative, coming King, creative, comforting, close, committed, challenging, cool, commendable, and consistent!

Appendix B

An Example of Promises

- You will fulfill your purpose for me.
- You will supply all my needs according to your riches in glory.
- You are with me to the ends of the earth.
- As I abide in you and your word abides in me I will bear much fruit.
- I will lay hands on the sick and they will recover.
- I will find You as I search for You with my whole heart.
- I will reap of the Spirit as I sow to the Spirit.
- Those who seek You and those who walk in righteousness will be filled with joy.
- Nothing can separate me from the love of God.
- Just as I am saved by grace I live in grace.

Appendix C

Some of My Crafted Prayers

A Prayer for JOY

Father, I praise you because:

You are a God of great joy! Jesus had on Him the oil of JOY more than anyone else.

The Gospel is Good News of great joy!

You delight in sharing Your joy with us. It is Your good pleasure to give us pleasure.

You and You alone are the source of the complete joy for which I and everyone else longs.

I have tasted of this inexpressible, eternal, and glorious joy. My life is a continual feast.

You have turned my mourning into joyful dance.

The life of the godly is full of light and joy(Proverbs 13:9).

You have given me greater joy than those who have abundant harvests of grain and new wine (Psalm 4:7-8).

I choose to find my joy in You today. No matter how I feel, nor how pleasing or awful my circumstances are, I will set my heart being happy in You. I will be glad and rejoice in your unfailing love (Psalm 31:7).

Please fill me with supernatural, abundant joy today as I:

- Lavish upon you exuberant adoration and the praise You so deserve.
- Overflow with gratitude toward You and others.

- Love and invest in the lives of others who become my joy in You.
- Welcome every trial and hardship as an opportunity for great joy.
- Surrender everything to You knowing that I will only truly find my life through losing it.
- Ask and receive the longings of my heart.
- Delight in quick, complete, and radical obedience to Your will.
- Choose to identify with the sufferings of Christ.

Please pour out Your oil of joy on me (Psalm 45:7). Satisfy me this morning with Your unfailing love that I might sing for joy throughout this day. In every interaction and every situation may Your joy be evident in me through warm smiles, fun remarks and gestures and a winsomeness that communicates how deeply satisfied I am in You. Help me find more and more things to laugh about.

A Prayer to Grow in Love

Father, I open my heart for a fresh revelation of Your love for me today. May I be rooted and established in that love. May I know how high, and wide, and long, and deep is Your love for me. Let know it, not only in my head, but in my heart—to experience it—to feel it. I open my heart to receive all the love Your Holy Spirit can pour out in me. Your fatherly, proactive, kind, unconditional, corrective, and transforming love. I receive today's portion of Your unfailing love. Would you surprise me with new expressions of your love? "Show me your unfailing love in wonderful ways" (Psalm 17:7). May You lead my heart into a full understanding and expression of the love of God that comes from Christ (2 Thessalonians 3:5).

Let this love, in turn, overflow into the lives of others today. Let Your agape love consume me, control me, compel me, and urge me on (2 Corinthians. 5:14). Love through me, everyone I encounter today. Help me to:

- Cloth myself in LOVE.
- Make LOVE the priority of my life—the main thing.
- Follow that divine flow of compassion.
- Be controlled by the love of Christ.

Please help me do LOVE by …

- Discerning the heart needs of others and respond to those needs quickly, purposefully, and sincerely.
- Placing the needs of others above my own, consistently willing to give up "my" rights in order to love.
- Purposefully expressing love from my heart, not dolling it out in small portions but extravagantly, generously, like You did for us through Jesus Christ.
- Acts, words, and attitudes of kindness and compassion.

Transform my heart to love with greater sincerity, greater consistency, and greater capacity. At the very core of my being, the fullness of my heart, may my response to everyone be kindness, patience, longsuffering, compassion, and tenderness. May I not be easily angered, envious, proud, boastful, or rude. I choose to quickly forgive and release the offenses of others who hurt me today. Empower me to intentionally love everyone I encounter today, especially those who are most unlovely, even my enemies.

Love through me the person in front of me. May your compassion be evident on my face, in my eyes, in my smile, in the words I say.

Please bring Your Love to full expression in me.
May I overflow with this love more and more!
Amen.

Appendix D

My True Identity in Christ
Examples

By the death and resurrection of Jesus Christ and the sanctifying work of the Holy Spirit I am:

1. Blessed with every spiritual blessing in Christ Jesus (Ephesians 1:3).

2. Chosen in Him before the creation of the world (Ephesians 1:4; 1 Peter 2:9).

3. Made holy in Jesus Christ (1 Corinthians 1:2).

4. A son of God (Romans 8:15).

5. A slave to righteousness (Romans 6:18).

6. Free from the controlling power of sin (Romans 6:6-7).

7. God's workmanship—His masterpiece (Ephesians 2:10).

8. Destined to do good works which God has prepared for me (Ephesians 2:10).

9. Near to God, by the blood of Jesus Christ (Ephesians 2:13).

10. God's possession—I belong to Him (2 Corinthians 5:14-15; 1 Peter 2:9; 1 Timothy 6:11).

11. A new person and new creation (2 Corinthians 5:17).

12. Dead to the flesh—the old pattern of living (Romans 6:3,7).

13. More than a conqueror through Him who loves me (Romans 8:37).

14. God's witness—even to the ends of the earth (Acts 1:8).

15. God's friend (John 15:15-16).

16. Able to do all things through Him who gives me strength (Philippians4:13).

17. Loved by God, the object of His compassion (John 16:27; Romans 8:37).

18. Righteous—in right standing with God (Romans 5:19).

19. Not of this world—I am a foreigner and alien (1 Peter 1:17).

20. A priest (1 Peter 2:9).

21. A member of His household—His family (1 Peter 2:9-).

22. The salt of the earth (Matthew 5:13).

23. The light of the world (Matthew 5:14).

24. Complete—I have everything I need for living a godly life (2 Peter 1:3).

25. Able to say "no" to temptation, ungodliness, and worldly passions (1 Corinthians 10:13; Titus 2:12).

26. An overcomer—because greater is He who is in me than he who is in the world (1 John 4:4; 5:4).

27. A fisher of men (Matthew 4:19).

28. A member of the body of Christ (1 Corinthians 12:13, 27).

29. A slave to Jesus Christ (Jude 1).

30. An ambassador of Christ Jesus (2 Corinthians 5:20).

31. Alive with life that is truly life (Romans 6:11; Ephesians 2:4-5).

32. Seated with Christ in heavenly places (Ephesians 2:6).

33. Given a new heart—a good and noble heart
    (Ezekiel 36:26; Luke 8:15).

34. I live in the love of God and the care of Jesus Christ.
    (Jude 1).

35. I am fearfully and wonderfully made (Psalm 139).

36. I am a life-giving fragrance to those being saved
    (1 Corinthians 2:16).

37. I am set free from the evil powers of this world
    (Colossians 2:20).

38. I am the recipient of every good thing—every gracious
    gift that the Lord provides (Psalm 84:11).

39. Your hand of blessing is upon my head (Psalm 139:5b).

40. Never far from you, wherever I go (Psalm 139:5a,8).

To order additional copies

To order more copies of *Building Your Spiritual Core: 101 Creative Ways to Connect with God* at a discount rate

Contact

ronindo@me.com

or call 512.914.9301